WOOD PELLET
SMOKER AND GRILL
Cookbook

Contents

Appetizers and Sides

Poultry Recipes

Beef Recipes

Pork Recipes

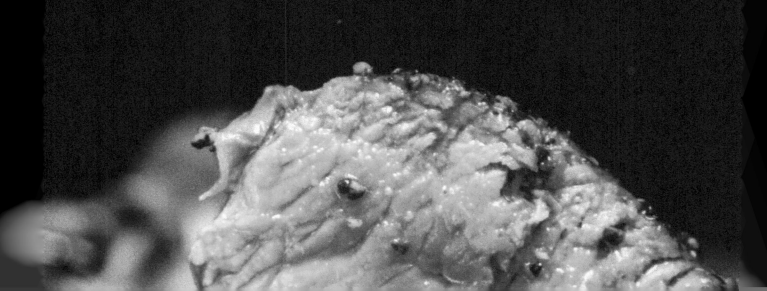

Cocktail Recipes

Vegetarian Recipes

Seafood Recipes

WHAT IS WOOD PELLET SMOKER AND GRILL?

To feed wood pellets into the smoker, wood pellet smokers and grills use an electronically operated thermostat and feeding device. This enables the smoker, by adding wood as necessary, to maintain an even, predictable heat.

The wood pellets made for smokers are healthy for food and can be had in a range of wood types and flavors to suit the foods being smoked or grilled, unlike pellet stoves.

WHY WOULD YOU LIKE TO COOK WITH WOOD PELLET SMOKERS?

Wood pellet smokers are absolutely awesome as you can roast, bake, smoke and barbecue with them, fueled by hardwood pellets, which serve as both a flavor enhancer and also a fuel for cooking food. They are very simple to use and they also automatically maintain the optimal cooking temperature for hours. As the technique of indirect cooking is used, the food cooked on them is very delicious and they are therefore much healthier than food cooked on charcoal smokers and gas.

HOW DO WOOD PELLET SMOKERS AND GRILLS WORK?

The grill runs on electricity itself and is plugged for power into an outlet. This auger then drives pellets into the firepot at a pace and time set by the temperature control panel. Pellets are applied to the hopper and funneled down to a spinning auger and motor. An igniter rod produces a flame when they hit the firepot and smoke is produced. A fan blows up at the bottom of the firepot and spreads heat and smoke across the grill's body, adding the cooking style of convection to your meal.

THE FABULOUS MERITS OFFERED BY WOOD PELLET SMOKERS?

Users can barbecue, grill, roast, smoke, still bake and braise in wood pellet smokers, being useful in many applications.

They are built in such a way that they are absolutely discouraged from fire fare ups and preheat pretty quickly, like in almost 10-15 minutes.

Indirect cooking is the cooking technique used in them. This implies that only the heat between the smoker and the food is used for the purposes of cooking. Often, no extra heat comes from the smoker's bottom and top. As opposed to gas and charcoal smokers, the foods cooked on these smokers are much tastier due to indirect cooking technique.

In wood pellet smokers, the option of temperature control is available. This helps to give heat control to the cooker position. In the cooking chamber, the presence of a thermostat aids direct signals and controls the distribution of pellets.

They provide the food with an incredible smoky wood taste. The use of various wood pellets gives the food a different smoky flavor. Maple, plum, alder, pecan, hickory, mesquite etc. are several distinct types of pellets.

Since they contain a lot less carcinogens compared to traditional smokers, the food cooked

STARTING EASY

The advantage of a smoker grill for wood pellets is that they are part grill, part smoker, part oven and can withstand anything you want to throw at them. If you've never been around one or cooked one, they can be a little daunting, but as soon as you get a couple of cooks under your belt, you'll learn to rely on their reliability.

I like to suggest that pellet grills with the flavor advantages of cooking over wood are the ease of a gas grill.

WHAT COAL IS SUITABLE FOR SMOKING?

A smoker is normally powered by wood when it comes to fuel. The grilled food's traditional smoked flavor is the product of the individual scent of the pieces of wood. This can also be varied, incidentally, depending on which wood is used. It is important that you do not use wood that is too resinous, such as pine or fir, while working with wood, seeing as these woods smoke a lot and can make food bitter.

You can also fire your smoker with charcoal if you like, and with a few smoking chips, add the smoky flavor. You certainly should go by the smoker's size. The bigger the smoker, the thicker the walls, and the more difficult it is with coal to maintain the temperature.

Pellet Grill Smokers Issues & Problems (Troubleshooting & Tips)

Anything with a bit of technology would have problems and issues to contend with, including pellet grills.

To start with, here is a short overview of the power pellet grill's bare bone main electrical components.

Pellet Grill Main Electrical Components:
Fan (or Fans)
RTD (Sensor for Temperature)
Auger & Motor (Feeds the Pellets with a Screw Mechanism)
Computer (Thermostat Control etc ..)
Igniter (Hot Rod)
It's not really that difficult if you're not familiar with the electrical components of a pellet grill. It's all about how they work together to have a seamless system of activity.

If you're a little short of time, to start with, here are the most helpful tips I have that will avoid most of these common problems. It's the old slogan for your pellet grill, about a bit of TLC (Tender Loving Care) that will really make it a smoother ride.

A Pellet Grill Tips to Prevent Problems:
Regularly substitute wood pellets
Don't leave pellets of wood on the grill

After each cooker, clean the temperature probe
Regularly Empty Ash, Keep the burn pot clean
Yeah, I know, pretty obvious things, but the number of times I hear about one of these common problems below, one of the above maintenance aspects is too often not completed.

Common Pellet Grill Problems:
Your Pellet Grill Technical Issues
Before you start poking around with some of these technical or performance problems, please remember to turn off and unplug the pellet grill. Yeah , I know common sense, but it's always worth noting.
Computer / Display Switch On
Jams Auger from the Pellets
Not Igniting Pellet Grill
During cooking, fire leaves
Induction Fan Not Working
Tripping / Circuit Breaker Keeps GFCI
Display / Computer Does Not Turn On

First of all, the obvious responses are to verify that it is plugged in and that the GFCI (Ground Fault Circuit Interrupter) or circuit breaker does not trip. So the electric juice flows to the starter pellet grill.
If the fuse is off, check the pellet grill fuse-the hot rod is most often on the way out or damaged in some way and needs replacement.

HOW TO CLEAN AND MAINTAIN YOUR SMOKER GRILL

Routine maintenance can keep your smoker in good condition with regular usage and proper storage. The more you keep the outside clean and the seasoned inside, the longer it will last and it will work better.

INSTRUCTIONS

MAINTENANCE ON ROUTINE:
1. After each use, remove the ashes. Ash is moist and can form by-products that facilitate rusting. Let the ashes cool completely, sweep them out and dispose of them in a metal container that is airtight.
2. Using a wet damp cloth to clean spilled sauces or marinades off the surfaces.
3. Before using a nylon bristle wipe, brush off the grates.
4. To scrape out any grease or bits of food in the cooking chamber, use a 4 "putty knife.
5. Buff them out with steel wool for any spots that begin to show rust and re-season them with beef tallow or other high-temperature cooking oil.
HOT TIP: Use canola oil spray in a pinch. It's not as comprehensive as a complete

re-seasoning, but a tiny rust spot is better than avoiding it.

DEEP Washing / REHAB CLEANING:

1. It is a good idea to rehabilitate the smoker with a deep cleaning after a lot of "deferred care" or a long time of sitting idle. Leave the inside of the cooking chamber alone to preserve the seasoning, if necessary. But occasionally, from scratch, you'll have to start again.

2. Do a burn that is clean (optional). This will burn out some of the waste and it will be easier to deal with whatever is left behind. Load the coal basket, light the fire and let the vents rip wide open with it. Make sure that the smoker is away from any combustible materials during this process and keep an eye on it. Before moving to the next step, let the smoker completely cool.

3. Wash the smoker with hot water and detergent with a degreaser. Rinse thoroughly and air dry.

4. Treat spots with rust. To avoid any deep rust or pitting, use a wire brush. Burnish over with fine metal or steel wool sandpaper when removed. Spray paint over the area with high-temperature paint for exterior surfaces.

5. Test the calibration of your thermometer. Stick the stem in boiling water and see if your elevation reads the right boiling point (about 212 ° F). By turning the nut at the rear of the thermometer until it reads the correct temperature, many thermometers are adjustable.

6. The smoker's re-season. With beef tallow, lard or other high-temperature cooking oil, scrub down all surfaces, inside and out. Create a fire and run the smoker for a few hours at 350 ° F.

WHICH RECIPES AM I SUPPOSED TO USE?

At the start, we have a few simple recipes for you that you can quickly get started with, even as a beginner. There's plenty for everyone here, whether it's spare ribs, roast, or something more special, such as trout or duck. What we highly suggest to you: get yourself a meat thermometer and look for the various pieces of meat at the appropriate core temperatures. So, you already know how to grill your food and you can shorten or lengthen the preparation time or change the temperature if appropriate. You can certainly be confident with a thermometer that you can find the right temperature for the different pieces. But because not everyone has a thermometer at home, the core temperatures from the recipes have been purposely left out. And you can get into the subject of smokers slowly and you can really get started when you have a meat thermometer. But the first thing is now: invite your friends or family, heat up the smoker, and you're ready to go!

Check Out The Best 100 Healthy Wood Pellet Smoker And Grill Recipes To Begin.

Appetizers and Sides Recipes

FOR WOOD PELLET SMOKER GRILLS

Smoked Blackberry
Popsicle with Mascarpone and Cookie Crunch

SERVING	PREP TIME	COOK TIME	PELLETS
6	15 MINS	25 MINS	MESQUITE

In the freezer section of your grocery store, you cannot find these popsicles. Before being frozen and finished off with a dip in our fresh baked cookie crunch, smoked blackberry puree meets a cool and creamy mascarpone combination.

INGREDIENTS:

6 Ounce blackberries
1/2 Cup sugar
1 lemon, juiced
Pinch salt
8 Ounce Cheese, mascarpone
2 Tablespoon heavy cream
1/4 Teaspoon Cardamom
1/2 Cup Nilla Wafers
1/4 Cup butter, melted
2 Tablespoon granulated sugar
1 Tablespoon Nonfat Dry Milk Powder

DIRECTIONS:

Set the temperature to 180 F when ready to cook and preheat for 15 minutes with the lid closed. If available, use Super Smoke for the optimal flavor.

On a perforated sheet tray, spread the blackberries out and put them directly on the grill grate. For 15-20 minutes, smoke. Take it off the grill and let it cool. Move the sugar, lemon juice and a pinch of salt to a blender pitcher. If you like it a little chunky or puree all the way and strain out the solids for a smooth texture, pulse a few times to break up the berries. Only set aside.

Whisk the mascarpone, cream, cardamom and salt together in a medium bowl.

Scoop each mixture 1 tablespoon at a time in a popsicle mold until the mold is filled. Add the stick to the popsicle and pass it to the freezer. Overnight freeze.

For the cookie crunch: Mix the wafers, butter sugar and milk powder in the bowl of a food processor. To make a coarse crumble, pulse. On a parchment lined baking sheet, spread the mixture out.

Modify the temperature to 350 ° F.

Directly placed the sheet tray on the grill grate and bake for 10-15 minutes. Let cool at room temperature then break up a bit with your fingers.

Remove from the molding when the popsicles are frozen and dip into the cookie crumble. Enjoy! Enjoy!

Smoked Mashed Potatoes

SERVING	PREP TIME	COOK TIME	PELLETS
6	20 MINS	45 MINS	SIGNATURE PELLET BLEND

Smokin' delicious are these mashed potatoes. Boiled up until tender until sprinkling a spark of smoked butter and cream, baked on the Traeger for quite a crust.

INGREDIENTS:

2 Pound red bliss potatoes, washed and diced medium
As Needed chicken stock or water
1/2 Stick salted butter
1 Cup whole milk
1/2 Cup sour cream
1/2 Cup shredded or grated Parmesan cheese
To Taste kosher salt
To Taste freshly ground black pepper
1/2 Cup fresh sliced green onions

DIRECTIONS:

In a small saucepan or stockpot, put the diced red potatoes and cover them with chicken stock or water.
Bring to a boil and simmer until the fork is tender, then cook until soft for 4 to 5 minutes after that.
Set the Traeger temperature to 400 ° F when ready to cook and preheat, the lid closed for 15 minutes.
Add butter and milk to a separate ovenproof pan, such as a cast iron skillet, and position in the Traeger until melted during start-up (about 7 to 10 minutes).
Using heatproof gloves, extract the butter / milk mixture from the Traeger carefully.
Drain the potatoes, then put them in a big bowl. The melted butter / milk mixture is added and mashed slowly.
Add the sour cream, cheese and green onion and season with salt and pepper to taste.
Place the skillet back in the Traeger and cook until the potatoes have a slight crust and are bubbling, about 15 minutes. Place the skillet back in the Traeger.
Using heatproof gloves, remove the mashed potatoes from the Traeger carefully. Allow get cool for 5 minutes. Scoop and enjoy!

Smoked Mexican Hot Chocolate

SERVING	PREP TIME	COOK TIME	PELLETS
2	15 MINS	35 MINS	APPLE

This season, spice up your hot chocolate routine with our recipe for Smoked Chili Hot Chocolate. Sweet and spicy in one mug blends this winter favorite, keeping you warm with wood-fired flavor.

INGREDIENTS:

Units of Measurement:
1/8 Teaspoon cayenne pepper
1/2 Teaspoon ground cinnamon
1/2 Teaspoon smoked paprika
333/500 Cup heavy cream
4 Cup milk
1/2 Cup sugar
1/4 Cup cocoa powder
1/8 Teaspoon salt
1 3/4 Chocolate, Bittersweet
1/2 Teaspoon vanilla extract

DIRECTIONS:

When ready to cook, set the temperature of the grill to 180 ° F and preheat for 15 minutes, lid closed.
Smoke the cayenne pepper for approximately 30 minutes in a heatproof pan. In the grill, add the cinnamon and paprika and smoke for an additional 5 minutes.
Scald the milk, cream, and sugar in a medium saucepan. Whisk in the cocoa and salt after a couple of minutes.
Stir in the bittersweet chocolate, smoked spices, and vanilla once the mixture is warmed.
Whisk until mixed and serve with marshmallows or whipped cream. Enjoy! Enjoy!!

Homemade Onion Dip

SERVING	PREP TIME	COOK TIME	PELLETS
8	30 MINS	45 MINS	HICKORY

The caramelized onions on your Traeger are simple to produce. What makes this dip overly addictive is pulling out those sweet flavors. It's the best game-day block dip.

INGREDIENTS:

1 Tablespoon butter
1 Tablespoon vegetable oil
2 Large sweet onion
1 1/2 Teaspoon sugar
1 Teaspoon garlic salt
1 Teaspoon black pepper
1/2 Teaspoon dried thyme
1/2 Cup beef bouillon
1 Tablespoon Worcestershire sauce
1 Tablespoon bourbon
1 1/2 Cup sour cream
8 Ounce cream cheese
2 Tablespoon Chives, fresh

DIRECTIONS:

Set the grill temperature to 250 degrees when ready to cook, and preheat with the lid closed for 15 minutes.

In a disposable foil plate, place the butter and vegetable oil and place it on the grill grate. Stir in the onions (diced), sugar, garlic salt , pepper, and thyme when the butter is melted.

In a glass measuring cup, mix the beef bouillon, Worcestershire sauce, and bourbon if used, and pour half over the onions.

Return the pan to the grill and cook the onions until soft and golden brown (about 45 minutes to 1 hour), stirring occasionally, adding more sauce if appropriate. Let it absolutely cool the onions.

Combine the sour cream and cream cheese in a large mixing bowl while you are cooking the onions and stir until smooth.

If used, whisk in the cooled onions and chives. To taste, add more salt and pepper.

Cover before serving, and relax. Serve with pancakes or chips of potato. Enjoy! Enjoy!

Smoked Macaroni Salad

SERVING	PREP TIME	COOK TIME	PELLETS
4	3 HOURS	20 MINS	HICKORY

For a summer classic, try this smoky twist. Macaroni is boiled and smoked and mixed together in a tangy dressing with red onions, green bell peppers and shredded carrots.

INGREDIENTS:

1 Pound macaroni, uncooked
1/2 Small red onion, diced
1 green bell pepper, diced
1/2 Cup shredded carrot
1 Cup mayonnaise
3 Tablespoon white wine vinegar
2 Tablespoon sugar
To Taste salt
To Taste black pepper

DIRECTIONS:

Bring to a boil a large stock pot of salted water over medium heat and cook pasta as instructed by the packet. Be sure to prepare, strain, and rinse under cold water for al dente.

Set the grill temperature to smoke and preheat when ready for cooking, with the lid closed for 15 minutes.

On a sheet tray, spread the cooked pasta and put the sheet tray directly on the burner grill. Smoke, detach from the heat and switch directly to the refrigerator to cool for 20 minutes.

Mix the dressing while the pasta is refrigerating. In a medium bowl, place all ingredients and whisk to mix.

Combine chopped vegetables, smoked pasta and dressing in a wide bowl if the pasta is cool.

Cover with plastic wrap and place for 20 minutes before serving in the refrigerator. Enjoy! Enjoy!

Smoked Whipped Cream

SERVING	PREP TIME	COOK TIME	PELLETS
4	7 HOURS	40 MINS	APPLE

Until whipping, cold-smoke cream to add an extra dollop of delicious to every dessert from Traegered.

INGREDIENTS:

3 Cup heavy cream
1/2 Cup sour cream
6 Tablespoon powdered sugar
1/2 Tablespoon vanilla extract

DIRECTIONS:

Set the temperature to 180° F when ready to cook and preheat for 15 minutes with the lid closed.
In an oven-safe dish or pan, add heavy cream into it. Do not use iron castings.
Place the cream on the Traeger grill and cook for 20 minutes on the smoke environment. To make the smoke taste better, smoke for 40 minutes.
Remove the Traeger's cream and let it sit for 1 hour at room temperature. Place it in the refrigerator for at least six hours. Place all the ingredients in the mixing bowl and apply the cream to the mixture. Only whisk until stiff peaks hit the milk.
Serve with your desserts or fruit favorites. Enjoy! Enjoy!

Smoked Deviled Eggs

SERVING	PREP TIME	COOK TIME	PELLETS
4	15 MINS	30 MINS	HICKORY

Kick this smokin 'starter off the festivities. To make it even better, we give this crowd-pleasing appetizer the Traeger treatment.

INGREDIENTS:

7 hard boiled eggs, cooked and peeled
3 Tablespoon mayonnaise
3 Teaspoon diced chives
1 Teaspoon brown mustard
1 Teaspoon apple cider vinegar
Dash hot sauce
To Taste salt and pepper
2 Tablespoon cooked bacon, crumbled
As Needed paprika

DIRECTIONS:

When ready to cook, set the temperature of the Traeger to 180 ° F and preheat for 15 minutes, lid closed. If available, use Super Smoke for the optimal flavor.
Directly put the cooked and peeled eggs on the grill and smoke the eggs for 30 minutes. Remove from the grill and leave to cool the eggs. Lengthwise, slice the eggs and scoop the egg yolks into a top bag with a gallon zip.
Combine the container with mayonnaise, chives, mustard, vinegar, hot sauce, salt , and pepper. Zip the bag closed and knead all the ingredients together, using your fingertips, until absolutely smooth.
Squeeze one corner of the bag with the yolk mixture and cut off a small section of the corner. Pipe the yolk mixture into the egg whites that are hard-boiled. Cover with crumbled bacon and paprika over the deviled eggs. Chill until it's ready for serving. Enjoy! Enjoy!

Smoked Banana Pudding

SERVING	PREP TIME	COOK TIME	PELLETS
4	15 MINS	30 MINS	OAK

Layered into creamy pudding and wafers, warm, syrupy, and slightly smoky brown sugar bananas make a banana pudding like you've never had before.

INGREDIENTS:

Units of Measurement:
4 Whole eggs
1/2 Cup sugar
3 Tablespoon all-purpose flour
1/2 Teaspoon salt
2 Cup milk
1/2 Teaspoon vanilla extract
4 Whole Bananas
2 Tablespoon butter
1/2 Cup whiskey
20 Nilla Wafers

DIRECTIONS:

Pudding: Remove the yolks from the three eggs and add the remainder of the whole egg to the yolks. Until smooth, whisk. Whisk together half a cup of sugar, flour, milk, and salt in a saucepan. Bring to a gentle boil, then simmer with less heat.

Scoop a bit of the hot milk mixture when whisking the eggs, then slowly pour it into the eggs. When the eggs are warmed, add the remaining milk into the pan with the egg mixture. Cook until thick (roughly 8-10 minutes) over medium heat. Remove the pudding and add vanilla from the heat.

Set the Traeger to high and preheat when ready for cooking, with the lid closed for 15 minutes.

Place on the grill and warm a medium cast iron pan. Add the butter and bananas and saute until the bananas are lightly browned, once the pan is heated. Be careful not to push them too far, or they're going to get mushy and fall apart.

Sprinkle with brown sugar once the bananas are browned and swirl to allow the sugar to melt. Remove the cast iron from the heat when the sugar is melted and whiskey is added. Return the pan to the grill and reduce the liquid until it is filled with syrup and bananas. This is expected to only take a few minutes.

To assemble, put in the bottom of a mason jar a few tablespoons of pudding, top with banana mixture and a bit of Nilla wafers. Repeat the process of layering until you have filled the pot.

Finish with a whipped cream dollop and serve. Enjoy! Enjoy!

Smoked Sweet & Spicy Cashews

SERVING	PREP TIME	COOK TIME	PELLETS
6	15 MINS	1 HOUR	HICKORY

For those sweet and spicy cashews, you'll go crazy. One addictive snack is red pepper chili flakes, fresh rosemary, and Smoked Simple Syrup.

INGREDIENTS:

3 Tablespoon Sambal oelek
1 Tablespoon Traeger Smoked Simple Syrup
1 Whole lemon zest
1/2 Tablespoon fresh rosemary
1 Teaspoon red pepper flakes
1/4 Teaspoon cayenne powder

DIRECTIONS:

Set the temperature to 225 ° F when ready to cook and preheat for 15 minutes with the lid closed. If available, use Super Smoke for the optimal flavor.

Sambal, simple syrup, lemon zest, rosemary, red pepper flakes, and cayenne are mixed in a small cup. Pour the mixture over the cashews and cover with a toss.

On a sheet tray, spread the cashews out and put them directly on the grill grill. Cook the nuts for 1 hour, sometimes stirring.

Remove and let cool from the grill. Enjoy! Enjoy!

Traeger Cajun Broil

SERVING	PREP TIME	COOK TIME	PELLETS
8	30 MINS	1 HOUR	PECAN

The Traeger is all grilled with bacon, potatoes, corn, and shrimp, and tossed together for a broil so tasty that you won't soon forget.

INGREDIENTS:

2 Tablespoon olive oil
2 Pound red potatoes
To Taste Old Bay Seasoning
6 Corn Ears, each cut into thirds
2 Pound smoked kielbasa sausage
3 Pound large shrimp with tails, deveined
2 Tablespoon butter

DIRECTIONS:

When ready to cook, set the temperature of the Traeger to 450 ° F and preheat for 15 minutes, lid closed.

Sprinkle the potatoes with half the olive oil, then season lightly with the Old Bay seasoning. Put it directly on the grill. Roast for 20 minutes or until soft.

Drizzle the remaining olive oil with the corn and season lightly with the Old Bay seasoning. Place the corn and kielbasa next to the potatoes directly on the grill grate. Roast for fifteen minutes.

Shrimp seasoning with Old Bay seasoning. Place shrimp next to the rest of the products directly on the grill grate and cook for 10 minutes, or until bright pink and cooked through. Remove and shift everything from the grill to a large bowl. With more Old Bay seasoning to taste, add butter and season. Toss to coat, then instantly serve. Enjoy! Enjoy!

Baked Hasselback Apples

SERVING	PREP TIME	COOK TIME	PELLETS
4	20 MINS	55 MINS	APPLE

This accordion-style dessert is going to have you singing all day long about Traeger's wood-fired flavor. And, when slicing the apples, here's a pro tip-placing wooden skewers on either side of the apples when slicing. At the skewers, the knife will stop and the slices will be the very same size.

INGREDIENTS:

3 Apples, pink lady or honeycrisp
5 Tablespoon butter, divided
5 Tablespoon brown sugar, divided
3/4 Teaspoon Ground Cinnamon, divided
2 Tablespoon flour
2 Tablespoon rolled oats
Pinch salt
To Taste Vanilla Ice Cream
To Taste caramel sauce

DIRECTIONS:

Peel the apples and use a melon baller to remove the core.
Halve the apples through the stem vertically and slice into 1/4-inch slices that end just before you get to the rim, leaving the slices intact.
When ready to cook, set the temperature of the grill to 400 ° F and preheat for 15 minutes, lid closed.
Melt 2 Tbsp of butter and mix with 1/2 tsp of cinnamon and 2 Tbsp of brown sugar.
In a baking dish, put the apples cut side down and brush the tops with the butter mixture.
Tightly cover the baking dish with foil and put directly on the barbecue grill. Bake for 30 minutes with the apples.
Take the grill out of the dish, remove the foil and let it cool for 10 minutes.
In a small bowl, blend the remaining sugar, butter, cinnamon, flour, oats and a pinch of salt together. Top each apple by pressing it between the layers with the oat mixture.
Return the baking dish to the grill and cook for an additional 15 minutes or until lightly browned with the oat topping.
Remove from the grill and let cool before serving for 5 minutes. To serve, top each apple with a scoop of ice cream and caramel sauce if desired. Enjoy!

Traeger Chex Party Mix

SERVING	PREP TIME	COOK TIME	PELLETS
8	15 MINS	1 HOUR	HICKORY

Give this savory holiday snack a rest & reach for your sweet tooth.

INGREDIENTS:

6 Tablespoon butter
2 Tablespoon Worcestershire sauce
1 1/2 Teaspoon seasoned salt
3/4 Teaspoon garlic powder
1/2 Teaspoon onion powder
3 Cup Cereal, Corn Chex
3 Cup Cereal, Rice Chex
3 Cup Cereal, Wheat Chex
1 Cup Mixed Nuts, Toasted
1 Cup Pretzels, bite-size
1 Cup Bagel Chips, garlic or regular, broken into bite sized pieces

DIRECTIONS:

Set the grill temperature to 250 degrees F when ready to cook, and preheat, with the lid closed, for 10 to 15 minutes.
On the grill, melt the butter in a broad roasting pan. Stir in the seasonings and Worcestershire. Stir in the remaining ingredients progressively until evenly coated.
Cook for 1 hour at 250 degrees F, stirring every 15 minutes.
Spread to cool on a paper towel. Store in air tight containers or ziplock. Enjoy! Enjoy!

Diva Q'S Smoked Party Mix

SERVING	PREP TIME	COOK TIME	PELLETS
8	10 MINS	3 HOUR	HICKORY

The party mix of Diva Q is a smoky & tasty snack that the fistful will devour for family & friends. Serve it on game day, or bag it to offer a holiday treat to your neighbors.

INGREDIENTS:

1 Box Cheerios cereal
1 Box Life cereal
2 Boxes Shreddies or Chex cereal
2 Boxes Cheez-Its or Cheddar Goldfish
2 Pound Pretzel Sticks
2 Pound smoked peanuts
1 Pound smoked almonds
1 Pound smoked pecans
1 Cup peanut oil
1 Cup clarified butter
2 Teaspoon granulated garlic
2 Teaspoon granulated onion
2 Teaspoon Lawry's Seasoned Salt
1/8 Cup Worcestershire sauce

DIRECTIONS:

Mix all the dry products together, then brush on the topping, ensuring that as much of the dry goods as possible is coated. Pour in two large aluminum pans that are disposable.
Set the Traeger temperature to 250 ° F when ready to cook and preheat, with the lid closed for 15 minutes.
For 2 to 3 hours, smoke the blend, turning every 15 minutes.
Remove and cool slightly from the grill. Enjoy! Enjoy!

Poultry Recipes

FOR WOOD PELLET SMOKER GRILLS

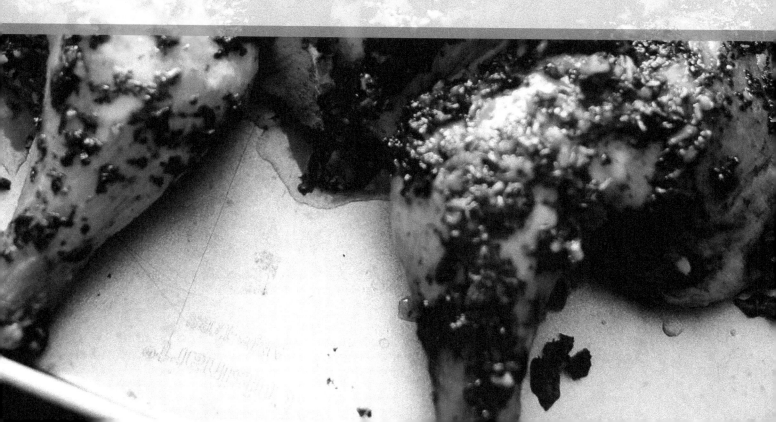

Smoked Cherry Bomb Chicken

SERVING	PREP TIME	COOK TIME	PELLETS
4	20 MINS	2 HOURS	MESQUITE

It's just a matter of time before your taste buds erupt with happiness when you devour this hot & sweet Thai chicken.

INGREDIENTS:

1 Quart cold water
1/3 Cup kosher salt
1/2 Cup sugar
10 Ounce cherry tomatoes
3 habanero peppers, seeded
4 Clove garlic
1/2 Teaspoon ground allspice
4 chicken legs (thigh and drumstick)
1 1/2 Teaspoon thyme
1 Teaspoon ground cumin
1 Teaspoon black pepper
1/2 Teaspoon cayenne pepper
3 Tablespoon vegetable oil
1/2 Cup Thai sweet chile sauce

DIRECTIONS:

In a saucepan, mix the water, kosher salt and sugar over low heat; cook for 4 to 5 minutes until the sugar and salt dissolve. To cool to room temperature, set aside.

In a blender, mix the cherry tomatoes, habanero peppers, garlic and allspice with a mixture of salt and sugar until smooth.

Score the skin side of each piece of chicken about 1/8 inch deep 2 to 3 times. In a large bowl or lidded container, position the chicken bits. Pour the tomato brine over the pieces of chicken, ensuring that all the pieces are coated. And refrigerate for 4 to 6 hours.

Remove chicken pieces and transfer to a plate or baking sheet lined with paper towels. With more paper towels, Pat's chicken pieces dry. Start the Traeger on Smoke when ready to cook with the lid open until a fire is formed (4-5 minutes).

In a small bowl, blend the thyme, cumin, black pepper, cayenne pepper, and oil together.

Brush some thyme and oil mixture with each chicken piece. (Don't put too much oil on it or you'll end up with some serious flare-ups elsewhere!)

For 30 minutes to 1 hour, smoke the chicken on the Traeger grill grate.

Increase the temperature to 350 degrees F and proceed to roast the chicken for approximately 50 to 60 minutes until the internal temperature in the thickest part of the thigh registers 165 degrees F on an instant-read meat thermometer.

On a tray, drop the chicken quarters and brush each piece with sweet Thai chili sauce. Move to a dish and allow the chicken to rest before serving for 10 minutes. Enjoy! Enjoy!

Whole Smoked Chicken

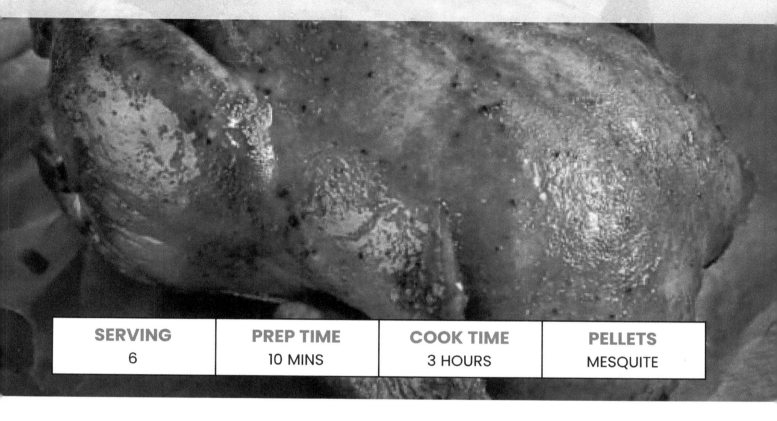

SERVING	PREP TIME	COOK TIME	PELLETS
6	10 MINS	3 HOURS	MESQUITE

Wrap your next cooked poultry with a little smoke. This whole chicken is brined, seasoned with our Big Game rub, smoked lemon, garlic, fresh thyme and mesquite for some smokin 'taste.

INGREDIENTS:

1/2 Cup kosher salt
1 Cup brown sugar
1 (3 to 3-1/2 lb) whole chicken
1 Teaspoon minced garlic
As Needed Traeger Big Game Rub
As Needed Traeger Big Game Ru
1 lemon, halved
1 Medium yellow onion, quartered
3 Whole garlic clove
5 thyme sprigs

DIRECTIONS:

For brine: In 1 gallon of water, dissolve the kosher salt and brown sugar. Place the chicken in the brine until dissolved, and refrigerate overnight. Make sure the chicken is completely submerged and, if necessary, weigh it down.

When ready to cook, set the temperature of the Traeger to 225 ° F and preheat for 15 minutes, lid closed. If available, use Super Smoke for the optimal flavor.

Remove the chicken from the brine and pat dry while the grill preheats. Rub with Traeger Large Game Rub and minced garlic. Next, stuff the lemon, onion , garlic and thyme in the cavity. Tie together the thighs.

When inserted into the thickest part of the breast, put the chicken directly on the grill grill and smoke for 2-1/2 to 3 hours or until an instant-read thermometer reads 160 ° F. The final internal temperature in the breast will increase to 165 ° F as the chicken rests. Until carving, let it rest for 15 minutes. Enjoy! Enjoy!

Smoked Buffalo Fries

SERVING	PREP TIME	COOK TIME	PELLETS
4	15 MINS	30 MINS	MESQUITE

Might we recommend a tangy alternative to smoking your fries — you'll know the buffalo smackdown is going on with these spicy fries..

INGREDIENTS:

4 Chicken Breast
As Needed sal
As Needed black pepper
2 Cup Blue Cheese Dressing
1/2 Cup Frank's RedHot Sauce
1 Celery, stalks
6 russet potatoes
As Needed Oil, For Frying

DIRECTIONS:

Set the Traeger to 325 ° F when ready to cook and preheat with the lid closed for 15 minutes.

Season the chicken breast with pepper and salt. For 25-30 minutes, or until 165 degrees, smoke. Set aside and pull.

In a mug, whisk together the blue cheese dressing and hot sauce; set aside.

In cold water, soak the cut celery (2' long sticks) until served.

Slice the potatoes into 1/4 sticks, similar to French fries.

In a Dutch oven or deep pot, heat oil to 375 degrees and put it gently into the potatoes. Drain on a sheet pan lined with paper towels. Fry until golden brown. Season with sea salt or kosher. Repeat until the potatoes have all been fried. In an oven, keep them warm until you are ready to eat.

Place the fries on a platter or wooden board lined with butcher paper to assemble. Drizzle the sauce mixture with the franks, then the pulled chicken. Garnish with celery and quickly serve. Enjoy! Enjoy!

Bacon-Wrapped Spatchcocked Turkey

INGREDIENTS:

1 (18-20 lb) fresh whole turkey
1 Traeger Orange Brine and Turkey Rub Kit
4 Tablespoon olive oil
1 1/2 Pound thick-cut applewood bacon

SERVING	PREP TIME	COOK TIME	PELLETS
10	20 MINS	2 HOURS	SIGNATURE PELLET BLEND

Wrap some serious flavor with your turkey in a bacon blanket to put on. This recipe is simple and delicious thanks to our Orange Brine and Turkey Rub pack.

DIRECTIONS:

Prepare the turkey by scraping the contents of the cavity and giblets under the front flap. Inside and out, clean the turkey, and set aside.

According to package instructions, prepare the Traeger Orange Brine and cool entirely.

Line a bucket with a brine bag and put the turkey in the brine bag carefully. Add the solution of brine and brine the turkey for 45 minutes per pound (under refrigeration).

Set the Traeger temperature to 190 ° F when ready to cook and preheat, the lid closed for 15 minutes. Take the turkey out of the brine carefully as Traeger heats up. NOT RINSE.

Place the turkey on a secure cutting board and cut along both sides of the backbone with heavy duty poultry shears or broad chef's knife, and remove the backbone. Be sure to look out for any bone shards and remove them.

Divide the breastbone / sternum and lay the turkey flat using poultry shears or the heel of your knife.

Rub the turkey with olive oil and season with Traeger Turkey Rub from the kit to taste.

Insert the turkey cavity / bone-side down into the Traeger and smoke for 1 hour at 190 ° F.

Make your bacon blanket on a sheet of butcher paper or foil while turkey is smoking. Keep cool.

Increase the Traeger temperature to 400 ° F after 1 hour of smoke, and preheat, with the lid closed for 15 minutes.

Open the lid and turn the bacon blanket over to the turkey carefully. NOTE: If you want to conserve gravy drippings, add turkey to a pan and cover it with a bacon blanket.

Add the Traeger WiFIRE probe to the thickest part of the breast and set a probe alarm for 160 ° F, for final internal temperature, carry over cooking will take turkey past 165 ° F.

Close the lid and let it cook for 1-1/2 to 2 hours with the turkey. Using heatproof gloves, remove the turkey from the Traeger carefully.

Remove the bacon blanket and save for the requirements for snacking or chopped bacon. Allow turkey to relax for 5 minutes, cut and enjoy!

Traditional Smoked Thanksgiving Turkey

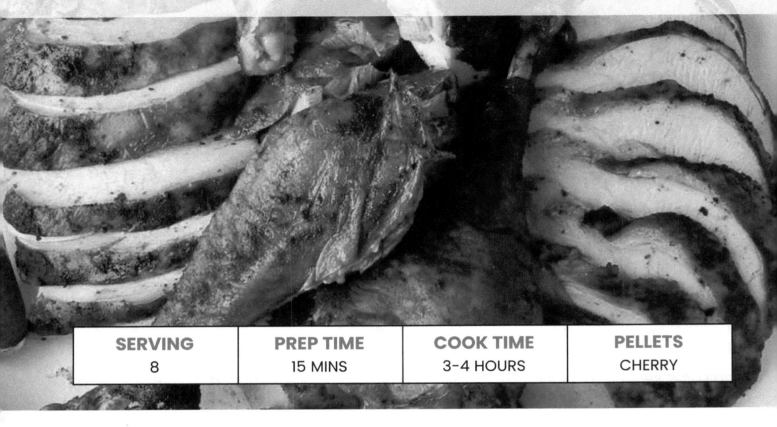

SERVING	PREP TIME	COOK TIME	PELLETS
8	15 MINS	3-4 HOURS	CHERRY

Simple spices & primal wood-fired flavor are needed for the best Thanksgiving turkey recipe. Your formula for success is Traeger.

INGREDIENTS:

Units of Measurement:
1/2 Pound butter
6 Clove garlic, minced
8 Sprig fresh thyme
1 Sprig fresh rosemary
1 Tablespoon cracked black pepper
1/2 Tablespoon kosher salt
20 Pound Turkey, Whole Birds (18-20 lbs)

DIRECTIONS:

Set the temperature of the grill to 300 ° F and preheat it for 15 minutes with the lid closed.

Combine the softened butter and the minced garlic, thyme leaves, chopped rosemary, black pepper and kosher salt in a small bowl.

Prepare the turkey to create a pocket to stuff the butter-herb mixture in by removing the skin from the breast. Cover the whole breast with a 1/4 inch thick butter mixture.

With kosher salt and black pepper, season the whole turkey. Optional: with traditional stuffing recipe, stuff turkey cavity. Set the grill temperature to 300 ° F when ready to cook and preheat, lid closed for 15 minutes.

Put turkey on the grill and smoke for 3-4 hours. Check the internal temperature, in the thigh next to the bone, the ideal temperature is 175 ° F and in the breast 160 ° F. Once taken off the grill, Turkey will continue to cook to achieve a final breast temperature of 165 ° F.

Before serving, let it rest for 10-15 minutes. Enjoy!

Smoked and Braised Duck Legs

SERVING	PREP TIME	COOK TIME	PELLETS
4	8 HOURS	2 HOURS	BIG GAME BLEND

Rich, savory, and fatty, braised duck leg meat, much like pulled pork, will fall off the bone. Get ready for a flavored feast.

INGREDIENTS:

2 Tablespoon salt
2 Tablespoon black pepper
1 Tablespoon brown sugar
1/2 Tablespoon fresh thyme
6 Whole Duck Legs
As Needed vegetable oil
2 white or yellow onions
2 Carrots, fresh
2 Celery, stalks
4 garlic
2 dried bay leaves
1 Bunch fresh thyme
1 rosemary sprigs
2 Cup red wine
3 Quart Stock, Of Choice

DIRECTIONS:

Mix the salt , pepper, sugar, and thyme together the night before you intend on cooking. Clean your duck legs and brush with the mixture. Place the duck legs in a pan on a cooling rack and place them overnight in the fridge.

Remove the legs of the duck from the refrigerator, clean with cold water and dry with paper towels.

Set temperature to high when ready to cook and preheat, lid closed for 15 minutes.

Place a wide cast-iron pan on the grill and allow 15 to 20 minutes to preheat. Add enough oil to coat the pan's rim.

In the pan, put the duck legs skin side down, close the lid and cook for 10 to 15 minutes, or until the skin is crisp and colored with mahogany.

Flip over and cook an extra 5 minutes. Turn the duck legs back over so that the fat side faces up.

Connect all the flavours, red wine, and then enough stock to reach 3/4 of the way to the duck.

Turn the grill to 350 ° F and uncover the duck legs for 2 hours or until very tender.

Decrease the Traeger to 180 ° F for the last 20 minutes of cooking. Remove the duck legs from the platter and keep the tent warm with foil.

Strain the braising liquid into a saucepan to create a sauce and reduce it until slightly thickened.

To taste, season with salt and pepper. Serve with sauce, grilled carrots, radishes, spring onions or your choice of vegetables. Enjoy! Enjoy!

Bacon Wrapped Turkey Legs

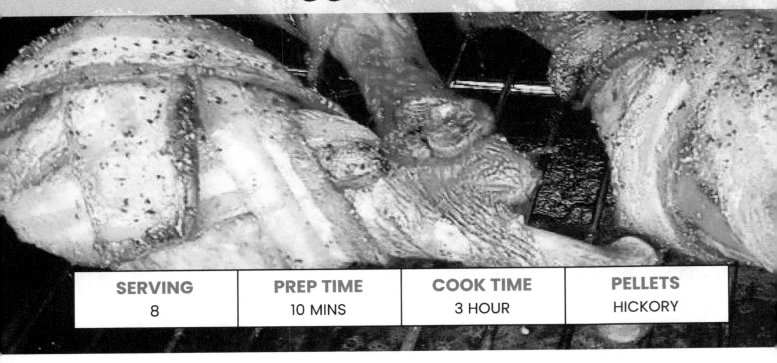

SERVING	PREP TIME	COOK TIME	PELLETS
8	10 MINS	3 HOUR	HICKORY

Colossal turkey legs are not just for the state fair, wood-fired turkey drumsticks are perfect for an intimate celebration.

INGREDIENTS:

Gallon water
To Taste Traeger Rub
1/2 Cup pink curing salt
1/2 Cup brown sugar
6 Whole peppercorns
2 Whole dried bay leaves
1/2 Gallon ice water
8 Whole turkey legs
16 Slices bacon

DIRECTIONS:

Combine one gallon of water, the rub, the soothing salt, brown sugar, peppercorns and bay leaves in a big stockpot. To dissolve the salt and sugar granules, bring them to a boil over high heat. Take the heat off and add 1/2 gallon of ice and water.

Make sure the brine is hotter, if not warmer, at least at room temperature. (The brine can need to be refrigerated for an hour or so.) Add the legs of the turkey, making sure they are fully immersed in the brine. Drain the turkey legs after 24 hours and discard the brine. With cold water, clean the brine off the thighs, then dry thoroughly with paper towels.

Start the Traeger barbecue according to grill instructions when ready to cook. Set the temperature to 250 degrees F and preheat for 10 to 15 minutes with the lid closed.

Lay the legs of the turkey directly on the grill grate.

For the last 30 to 40 minutes of smoking, wrap a piece of bacon around each leg after 2 1/2 hours and finish cooking them.

On an instant-read meat thermometer, the total smoking time will be 3 hours for the legs or until the internal temperature reaches 165 degrees F. Enjoy, serve!

Dry Brine Traeger Turkey

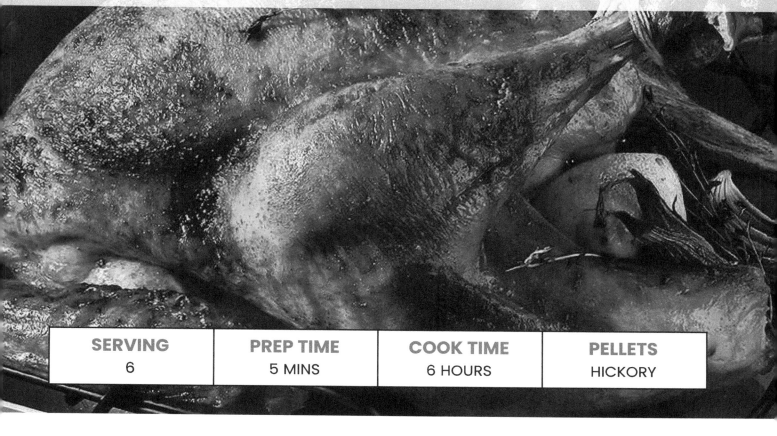

SERVING	PREP TIME	COOK TIME	PELLETS
6	5 MINS	6 HOURS	HICKORY

Jeffrey Potts gave the royal treatment to his winning 2015 Meat Madness turkey by brining it dry overnight for a super tender interior with a flavorful, toasted shell on the outside.

INGREDIENTS:

1 farm fresh turkey, any size
1 Teaspoon kosher salt per pound of turkey
As Needed fresh thyme
As Needed fresh rosemary
As Needed fresh sage
As Needed fresh parsley

DIRECTIONS:

Make sure this recipe needs several days of brine time to prepare ahead.

Combine the desired quantity of kosher salt with thyme, rosemary, sage, and/or parsley. Rubbing

Place the turkey in a plastic wrap or bag and seal it tightly. Place the turkey in the refrigerator for 2 days. Get the turkey out of the bag on day 3, or unwrap the plastic wrap. Put the turkey, uncovered for 24 hours, back in the fridge.

When ready to cook, set the temperature of the Traeger to 180 F and preheat for 15 minutes with the lid closed.

Put the turkey on the grill, breast up, breast up. Let the turkey smoke for 3 to 4 hours.

Increase the grill temperature to 325 ° F after 3 to 4 hours and continue cooking the turkey until it reaches an internal temperature of 165 ° F. Enjoy! Enjoy! Cooking time after smoking: 10 to 13 pounds 1-1/2 to 2-1/4 hours 14 to 23 pounds 2 to 3 hours 24-27 pounds 3 to 3-1/4 hours 28-30 pounds 3-1/2 to 4-1/2 hours 28-30 pounds 3-1/2 to 4-1/2 hours.

Smoked Thai Curry Chicken

SERVING	PREP TIME	COOK TIME	PELLETS
6	4 HOURS	20 MINS	ALDER

There is a special marinade in this sweet & spicy smoked Thai chicken curry recipe that will tantalize your taste buds.

INGREDIENTS:

1/4 Cup soy sauce
3 Tablespoon brown sugar
2 Tablespoon lime juice
2 Tablespoon extra-virgin olive oil
2 Teaspoon curry powder
1/2 Teaspoon Cardamom
2 Clove garlic, minced
1 Teaspoon Lemon Grass
1 Teaspoon freshly grated ginger
1 jalapeño, seeded and diced
As Needed Traeger Thai Red Curry Rub
3 Pound Chicken Breast
cilantro
Coconut

DIRECTIONS:

In a bowl, combine all the ingredients for the marinade (soy sauce, brown sugar, lime juice, oil, curry powder, cardamom, cloves, lemon grass, ginger, peppers, and red Thai curry rub). Pour the marinade along with the chicken breasts into a large resealable bag. Marinate the chicken for around 1-4 hours.

Set temperature to high when ready to cook and preheat, lid closed for 15 minutes.

Remove the chicken from the marinade and put it directly on the grill. Cook for approximately 10 minutes on either side or until an instant read thermometer reaches an internal temperature of 165 ° F.

Until serving, let the chicken rest for 5 minutes.

Garnish with cilantro and coconut flakes that are new. Enjoy! Enjoy!

Smoked Peppered Chicken

SERVING	PREP TIME	COOK TIME	PELLETS
6	10 MINS	1 HOUR	MESQUITE

Many like it hot! Try this spicy & smoky BBQ chicken recipe to spice up your life if you're bored with boring grilled chicken.

INGREDIENTS:

1 Cup Jalapeno Jelly
1 Cup water
4 chicken legs
As Needed Traeger Chicken Rub
As Needed chili powder

DIRECTIONS:

In a sauce pan, mix the jelly and water and boil on the stove top for around 10 minutes or until a medium-thick consistency is achieved.

With the chicken rub and chili powder, season the chicken parts.

Start the Traeger and preheat it for 10 to 15 minutes to 300 degrees F, with the lid closed.

Put the chicken on the grill and cook, with the lid closed, for 15 minutes.

Baste the pepper syrup on the chicken legs. Turn your legs over and baste them for 30 minutes every 15 minutes.

For 1 hour, turn the setting to Smoke and Smoke.

For the last 15 minutes, or until the chicken hits 165 degrees, turn back to 300 degrees F

Smoked Turkey with BBQ Sauce

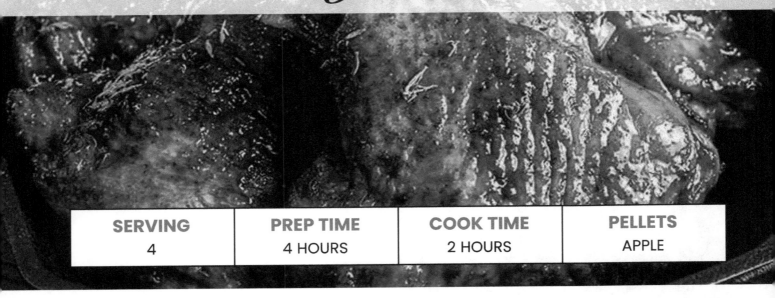

SERVING	PREP TIME	COOK TIME	PELLETS
4	4 HOURS	2 HOURS	APPLE

As tasty as they look, these brined turkey thighs are. Brined turkey thighs are rubbed with a rich and aromatic ras el hanout, smoked slowly and basted for deep color and flavor with a sweet fig bbq sauce.

INGREDIENTS:

1 Gallon water
1/2 Cup sugar
2 dried bay leaves
2 Large thyme sprigs
6 peppercorns
1/2 Cup salt
6 Turkey Thighs
1/2 Cup Ras El Hanout
6 Tablespoon extra-virgin olive oil
1 Cup Traeger Apricot BBQ Sauce
4 Figs, fresh

DIRECTIONS:

Bring the saline ingredients to a boil on the stovetop over high heat. Mix thoroughly until the sugar and salt are dissolved and let cool.

Attach the turkey thighs and let them brine for at least 4 hours or overnight. Remove, rinse and pat dry from the brine.

Set the temperature of the grill to 250 ° F and preheat for 15 minutes with the lid closed. If available, use Super Smoke for the optimal flavor.

Rub the turkey thighs with the ras el hanout, rub each of the olive oil with a tablespoon and then lay the thighs straight on the plate grill. 2 hours of smoking.

To make the fig BBQ sauce: In a small saucepan over medium heat, mix the figs (remove stems and cut into quarters) and Traeger Apricot BBQ Sauce. Add 3 tbsp of water and cook for 20 minutes, or add more water as required, until the figs have softened. Remove what remains and discard the figs.

Remove them from the grill when the turkey thighs have finished smoking and set the temperature to high and preheat for 15 minutes, lid closed. Add the thighs back and cook when the grill is to the temperature, basting regularly with the fig bbq sauce until deeply caramelized and the thighs have reached an inner temperature of 165 ° F.

Smoked Chicken with Chimichurri

SERVING	PREP TIME	COOK TIME	PELLETS
6	8 HOURS	45 MINS	ALDER

Chicken legs of smoked paprika, finished with a herby, spicy chimichurri sauce is a perfect way to enliven your chicken routine with savory flavor.

INGREDIENTS:

6 chicken legs
2 Tablespoon extra-virgin olive oil
1 Tablespoon paprika
1 Tablespoon Corriander Seeds, crushed in a mortar and pestle
lime zest
1 1/2 Teaspoon salt
1 Teaspoon black pepper
1 Cup fresh parsley
1 Cup cilantro leaves
1 jalapeño, seeded and halved
2 Medium Spanish onion, diced
3 Clove garlic clove
3 Tablespoon lime juice
2 Tablespoon red wine vinegar
1/3 Cup extra-virgin olive oil

DIRECTIONS:

Massage the chicken legs with olive oil, paprika, cilantro, lime zest, salt , and pepper in a large tub. Overnight, cover and marinade in the refrigerator for optimum deliciousness.

Set the temperature to high when ready to cook, and preheat the lid shut for 15 minutes.

Put the chicken directly, skin side up, on the pan grill. Cook for 40-45 minutes on an instant-read thermometer or until the chicken reads 165 ° F.

Note: This chimichurri recipe makes it great for grilled beef, fish, burgers, you name it, extra leftover goodness. Combine all ingredients in the base of a food processor to make the Chimichurri: and pulse until smooth & creamy.

Serve with the chimichurri on the grilled chicken legs, an extra squeeze of fresh lime juice and your favorite side dish. Enjoy! Enjoy! To read more about Pro Team member Chef Dennis Prescott, click here. Take the turkey thighs off the grill and baste them with a little more BBQ sauce. Enjoy! Enjoy!

Smoked Duck Breast Becon

SERVING	PREP TIME	COOK TIME	PELLETS
6	6 HOURS	2 HOURS	MAPLE

Nothing beats conventional bacon, before this recipe is tried out. In a sweet molasses and brown sugar mixture, these duck breasts are cured, smoked over sweet maple wood and thinly sliced for your new favorite meat candy. Tell hi to a handmade one.

INGREDIENTS:

4 Cup water
2 Cup Strong Brewed Coffee
1 Cup kosher salt
1/2 Cup dark brown sugar
2 1/2 Tablespoon curing salt
1/2 Cup molasses
3 Cup ice
6 Duck Breasts, skin on

DIRECTIONS:

In a cup with a lid, mix the water, coffee, kosher salt, brown sugar and soothing salt. Blend until the solids dissolve. Apply the molasses and stir until they dissolve fully. Add ice and swirl until the healing process is cold. It's okay if it doesn't absolutely melt all the ice.

To cure and weigh down with a large plate to hold submerged, add duck breasts. Put the covered container in a refrigerator for at least 6 hours.

Take the breasts out of the brine, remove them from the fridge and discard the brine. Rinse the duck breasts and pat dry under cold running water.

Set the temperature to 180 º F when ready to cook and preheat for 15 minutes with the lid closed. If available, use Super Smoke for the optimal flavor.

Put the duck breasts and smoke on the grill for 2 hours.

Absolutely cool the duck, wrap it in plastic wrap and put it in the refrigerator until ready for use. To cook, thinly slice the breast and fry it in a pan just like you would with bacon. Or slice thinly, put on a 350 º F grill and cook for 10 minutes on each side. Enjoy! Enjoy!

Beef Recipes

FOR WOOD PELLET SMOKER GRILLS

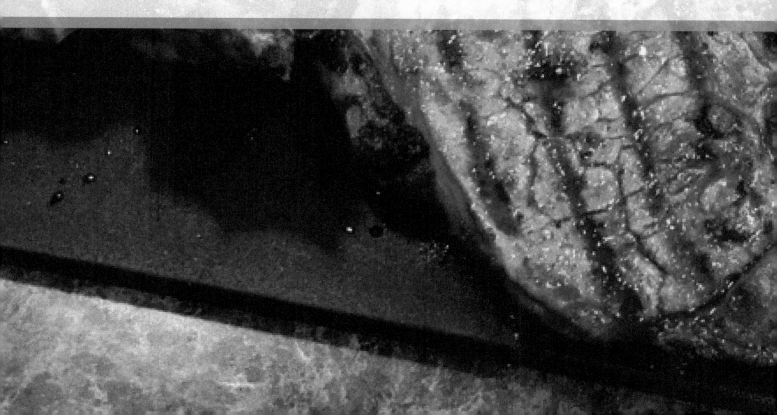

Short Rib Chili

SERVING	PREP TIME	COOK TIME	PELLETS
4	15 MINS	4 HOUR	MAPLE

Flavor runs so deep within that smokin 'chili. Savory short ribs are supplemented with rich, aromatic spices, spicy chiles, and a tasty brew. You haven't eaten this sort of chili before.

INGREDIENTS:

2 Whole dried ancho chiles, stemmed and seeded
2 Whole dried guajillo chiles, stemmed and seeded
2 Whole dried chile de arbol, stemmed and seeded
1 1/2 Quart chicken or beef stock
2 chipotle peppers in adobo, plus 2 teaspoons sauce from can
4 Pound boneless beef short ribs
To Taste salt and pepper
2 Tablespoon vegetable oil, plus more as needed
1 Large Spanish onion, diced
4 Clove garlic, chopped
1 jalapeño, finely chopped
1 cinnamon stick
2 bay leaves
1 Teaspoon Mexican oregano
1 Teaspoon roasted ground cumin
1 Teaspoon roasted ground coriander
1 Bottle beer
As Needed corn tortillas
cilantro, for serving
shredded cheddar cheese
sliced lime, for serving
chopped onion, for serving

DIRECTIONS:

When ready to cook, set the temperature of the Traeger to 225 ° F and preheat for 15 minutes, lid closed. If available, use Super Smoke for the optimal flavor.

Heat a skillet over medium heat on the stovetop and add the dried chiles. Toast in a dry skillet, occasionally tossing until fragrant, approx 5 minutes. Add a cup of stock to the pan, boil it immediately, and turn off the heat.

Along with the adobo chiles and their sauce, move the chiles and stock to a blender. Close the lid and allow steaming of the chiles before moving on to the next steps.

Season the short ribs generously with salt and pepper.

In a large Dutch oven, heat the vegetable oil on the stovetop over high heat until very hot. Sear the ribs until deeply browned on all sides, about 4 minutes per side. Do this in batches so that the pan is not overfull.

Remove the ribs from the board once seared and cut them into bite-sized cubes. (After searing, cutting the ribs results in less loss of moisture, making for a deeper sear and more tender meat.) Set aside the meat.

After the chiles have steamed with the stock, mix on high until smooth and set aside.

Lower the heat to low, and add more oil to the pan if necessary. Sauté the onions until soft, stirring occasionally, for 5 to 7 minutes. Apply the garlic, the chopped jalapeño, the cinnamon stick, the bay leaves, the oregano, the cumin and the coriander and mix until the spices begin to stick to the bottom of the pot for about a minute.

Pour in the beer and bring the bottom of the pan to a boil, scraping. Allow the beer to decrease by half and then stir in the chiles and stock blended. Add the short cut ribs back to the pot.

Pour in the stock until it is barely covered with the meat. Depending on the size of your Dutch oven, you will need to change the amount of stock used. Bring it to a boil, then carefully move the Traeger to the Dutch oven.

For around 3 hours, cook chili uncovered on the grill until the meat is exceedingly tender.

If needed, stir in 4 or 5 split up corn tortillas to help thicken the chili.

Also use cilantro, chopped onion, shredded cheddar cheese and lime to serve. Enjoy! Enjoy!

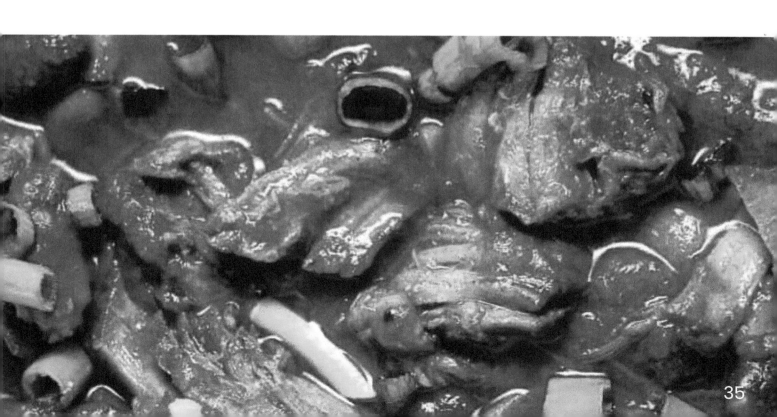

Smoked Elk Jerky

SERVING	PREP TIME	COOK TIME	PELLETS
4	30 MINS	30 HOUR	BIG GAME BLEND

Big game, with the wood-fired flavor of big time. This easy-to-make smoked elk jerky is absolutely wild for us.

INGREDIENTS:

1/2 Cup soy sauce
3 Tablespoon Traeger Jerky Rub
3 Tablespoon honey
1 Pound Elk Meat, Trimmed of Fat and Sliced Thin

DIRECTIONS:

For the marinade, whisk together the ingredients. In a Ziploc container, put the sliced meat in it. Pour the marinade over the meat and move it overnight (between 8-12 hours) to the fridge to marinate.

Remove the meat and discard the remaining marinade from the marinade.

Set the temperature to 180 ° F when ready to cook and preheat for 15 minutes with the lid closed.

Place the slices flat on the grill grate to ensure that they do not overlap. Close the lid and smoke the jerky until dry yet pliable for 4-6 hours. It will depend on the humidity in the air and the thickness of the elk slices for the time it takes.

Remove from the grill and allow to air dry for 1 hour or so. Store in the refrigerator in an air-tight jar. Enjoy! Enjoy!

Smoked BBQ Ribs

SERVING	PREP TIME	COOK TIME	PELLETS
4	25 MINS	5 HOURS	HICKORY

Heat up your Traeger and get the napkins out. These St. Louis-style ribs, smoky, saucy, and slightly sweet, are a cut above the remainder.

INGREDIENTS:

2 Rack St. Louis-style ribs
1/4 Cup Traeger Big Game Rub
1 Cup apple juice
Traeger BBQ Sauce

DIRECTIONS:

The membrane is dried and peeled from the back of the ribs by Pat ribs.

To the front, back and sides of the ribs, add an even layer of rub. If refrigerated, leave to sit for 20 minutes and up to 4 hours.

When ready to cook, set the temperature of the Traeger to 225 ° F and preheat for 15 minutes, lid closed. If available, use Super Smoke for the optimal flavor.

Place the ribs on a grill, bone side down. Put the apple juice in a spray bottle and, after 1 hour of preparation, spray the ribs. Afterwards, spray every 45 minutes.

Check the internal temperature of the ribs after around 4-1/2 hours. When the internal temperature reaches 201 ° F, ribs are made. Check back in another 30 minutes if not.

Brush a thin coating of your favorite Traeger BBQ Sauce on the front and back of the ribs as soon as the ribs are finished. For 10 minutes, let the sauce set. Take the ribs off the grill after the sauce has set and leave to rest for 10 minutes. Slice the ribs and serve with extra sauce in between the bones. Enjoy! Enjoy!

Smoked Baby Back Ribs

SERVING	PREP TIME	COOK TIME	PELLETS
6	15 MINS	3 HOURS	HICKORY

Looking for a quick and easy one? Make your new go-to recipe for these baby backs. To achieve a few serious meat sweats, all you need is a fresh rack, salt, pepper and a little hickory smoke.

INGREDIENTS:

3 Rack baby back ribs
To Taste kosher salt
To Taste cracked black pepper

DIRECTIONS:

Peel the membrane from behind the ribs and season with salt and pepper on both sides.
When ready to cook, set the temperature of the Traeger to 225 ° F and preheat for 15 minutes, lid closed. If available, use Super Smoke for the optimal flavor.
For two hours, cook the meat side up. Flip the ribs so that the side of the beef is down and cook for an extra hour. Enjoy! Enjoy!

Brined Smoked Brisket

SERVING	PREP TIME	COOK TIME	PELLETS
4	20 MINS	7 HOURS	MESQUITE

Low and slow means excellence of the brisket. Brined, seasoned generously with Traeger Beef Rub and grilled over mesquite for a smoked meat, this beef brisket is sure to elevate your BBQ game.

INGREDIENTS:

1 (5-7 lb) flat cut brisket
1 Cup brown sugar
1/2 Cup kosher salt
1/4 Cup Traeger Beef Rub

DIRECTIONS:

Dissolve 6 quarts of boiling water with salt and sugar. Then add 6 cups of ice and let it cool. Place the brisket and cover in the brine. Leave the brine overnight in the fridge.

Remove the brisket from the brine and use a paper towel to pat it dry. With Traeger Beef Rub, sprinkle uniformly.

Set the Traeger temperature to 250 ° F when ready to cook and preheat, with the lid closed for 15 minutes.

Place the brisket, fat cap down, and smoke for 3 hours on the Traeger.

Double cover the brisket in foil after 3 hours and turn the temperature up to 275 ° F. Cook the meat for around 3 to 4 hours until the internal temperature reaches 204 ° F.

Unwrap the brisket and put it on the grill for 30 more minutes, unwrapped.

Before slicing against the grain, remove the brisket from the grill and let it rest for 15 minutes. Enjoy! Enjoy!

Grilled Proterhouse Steak with Creamed Greens

SERVING	PREP TIME	COOK TIME	PELLETS
4	20 MINS	45 MINS	HICKORY

A King-fit Porterhouse. Reverse-seared for good measure and simply seasoned with creamy greens.

INGREDIENTS:

2 Steak, porterhouse
As Needed kosher salt
As Needed cracked black pepper
2 Tablespoon butter
2 Clove garlic, minced
1 shallot, thinly sliced
1 Cup heavy cream
1 Pinch ground nutmeg
4 Tablespoon butter
3 Pound Salad Greens, mixed

DIRECTIONS:

For the Steaks: Generously season each side with salt and pepper. Start the Traeger when it is ready to cook and set the temp to 225F and preheat for 10-15 minutes.

Put the steaks directly on the grill and cook for 45 minutes or until 120 degrees F. has reached the internal temperature.

Take the steaks off the grill and raise the temperature to 450-500F. Let the grill pre-heat for 10-15 minutes with the lid closed.

Return the steaks to the hot grill and cook on each side for 5-6 minutes, or until the internal temperature is 130 degrees F for medium rare. Take it off the grill and let it rest.

For the Creamed Greens: Heat 2 tablespoons of butter in a saucepan over high heat until the butter foams. Add the garlic and shallot and cook over medium-low heat, stirring for around 5 minutes, until golden and softened.

Add the milk, boil and cook for about 10 minutes, until slightly thickened. To taste, apply the nutmeg and salt. Purée until smooth, using a hand blender.

Heat the remaining 4 tablespoons of butter over high heat in a large pot, until it foams. Add the greens and cook, stirring constantly, for about 5 minutes, until tender but still bright green. Connect the cream mixture and sprinkle with salt. Reduce flame, cover and simmer until cooked through, for another 5 minutes. Taste the salt and nutmeg, season to taste and serve sweet.

Cut the steaks to serve and serve them on top of the greens. Enjoy! Enjoy!

Smoked German Rouladen

SERVING	PREP TIME	COOK TIME	PELLETS
4	25 MINS	2 HOURS	OAK

With a savory, crunchy dill pickle core, this traditional German dish blends thinly sliced beef. This will quickly become a new favourite, served with a soft, tasty gravy.

INGREDIENTS:

Units of Measurement:
2 Pound Beef, eye of round
4 Tablespoon Mustard, German stone ground
1 Pound thick-cut bacon
2 Large yellow onion, thinly sliced
1 Jar dill pickle spears
1 Teaspoon salt
1/2 Teaspoon cracked black pepper
2 1/2 Cup beef stock
1 Tablespoon Worcestershire sauce
1 Bay Leaf
2 Clove garlic, smashed
2 Tablespoon corn starch
4 Tablespoon cold water
1 Cup heavy cream

DIRECTIONS:

Using a meat mallet, put each slice of beef (1/4 inch thick) between 2 layers of plastic wrap and pound thinly. Spread evenly with 1/2 tablespoon of mustard on one side of each filet. On each steak, place the bacon, onions and pickle slices.

To shape a tight roll, wrap the steak around the bacon, pickles and onions. Keep the roll together using a string of toothpicks. Apply the salt and cracked black pepper to season.

Start the Traeger grill when you're ready to cook and set the temperature to 185 degrees F and preheat for 10-15 minutes. Place the rolls on the grill grate directly and smoke for 30 minutes. Close the lid and raise the temperature to 325 degrees by removing the steak rolls from the grill.

Enable the grill to preheat while the liquid for braising is being prepared. Combine the beef stock, Worcestershire sauce, bay leaf and cloves of smashed garlic in a large baking dish.

Put the steak rolls back on the grill and sear on each side (about 3-5 minutes per side).

Arrange the steak rolls gently in the liquid for braising and put the pan on the grill. Cook for 1 1/2-2 hours or until very tender for the steak. Remove the steak from the dish and cover it with tin foil on a different platter.

On the stove top, heat the baking dish. In a separate tub, combine the cornstarch and the cold water. In the baking dish, whisk the cornstarch mixture and cream slowly into the juices. Bring the gravy to a boil, stirring for 1-2 minutes, continuously.

Send the rolls back to the warm gravy and immediately serve. Enjoy! Enjoy!

Dry Brined Texas Beef Ribs

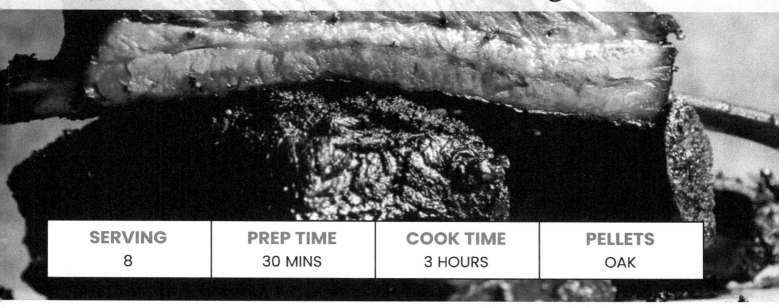

SERVING	PREP TIME	COOK TIME	PELLETS
8	30 MINS	3 HOURS	OAK

Do not let yourself be intimidated by these big ol 'beef ribs. This dry brine, quick to produce, takes 20 minutes to prepare and does much of the heavy lifting for you. Simply smoke and cover the ribs in foil for 4-5 hours after that, equivalent to a brisket. Smoke until 203 degrees F, and enjoy

INGREDIENTS:

12 beef short ribs
As Needed salt
As Needed Worcestershire sauce
As Needed Traeger Prime Rib Rub
As Needed Traeger Blackened Saskatchewan Rub
8 Ounce apple juice
8 Ounce beef stock

DIRECTIONS:

Purchase from your local grocer or butcher shop a box of uncut short ribs, recommended standard for Prime or Choice. For 2 racks of 4 bones each, typically 9-12 lbs for 8 total.

With a sharp knife, cut as much fat as possible from the top of the ribs. Take the membrane off the bottom of each 4-bone rack.

For a dry brine, sprinkle with kosher salt and seal in plastic wrap in your refrigerator for at least 6 hours or overnight.

Set the Traeger to 275 ° F when ready to cook and preheat, with the lid closed for 15 minutes.

Wipe from the top of the ribs the excess salt mixture. Before placing on a medium coat of Traeger Prime Rib, cover it with a light amount of Worcestershire sauce. Follow the Traeger Saskatchewan rub with a lighter coat. Sprinkle with apple juice and leave for 15-20 minutes to set.

Place the thicker portion of the ribs on the Traeger (if applicable) at the back of the grill. Smoke the ribs with a light spritz every 30 minutes for 4-5 hours to keep them moist until the inner temperature reaches around 180 ° F or the color has a good deep char.

For each rack of ribs, take the ribs off the grill like a brisket and cover them in 2 sheets of heavy duty foil along with 4 oz of broth. Put back on the smoker until the internal temperature of the meat is around 203 ° F for another 1 to 1-1/2 hours. Remove and slice. Immediately serve. Enjoy Enjoy!

Smoked Corned Beef Brisket

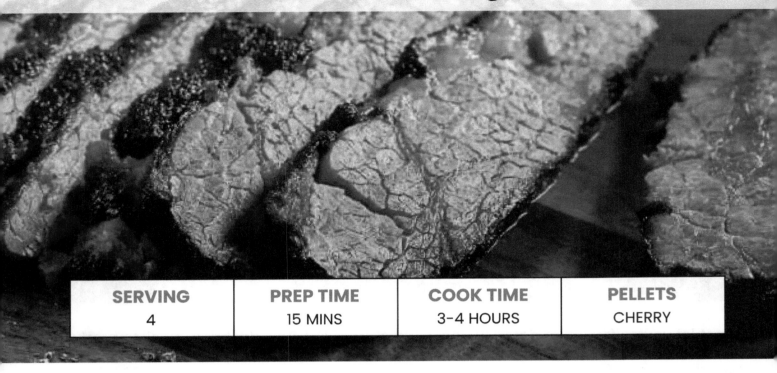

SERVING	PREP TIME	COOK TIME	PELLETS
4	15 MINS	3-4 HOURS	CHERRY

Right on the grill, toss brined corned beef and fire away. Grab your green beer; at the end of the rainbow, this brisket is gold.

INGREDIENTS:

1 (3 lb) flat cut corned beef brisket, fat cap at least 1/4 inch thick
1 Bottle Traeger Apricot BBQ Sauce
1/4 Cup Dijon mustard

DIRECTIONS:

Remove the brisket of corned beef from its packaging and discard, if any, the spice package. For at least 8 hours, soak the corned beef in water and change the water every 2 hours.

When ready to cook, set the temperature of the Traeger to 275 ° F and preheat for 15 minutes, lid closed.

Directly put the brisket on the pan grill, fat side up, and cook for 2 hours.

Meanwhile, in a medium cup, mix the Traeger Apricot BBQ Sauce and the Dijon mustard, whisking to combine.

In a disposable aluminum foil tray, pour half of the BBQ sauce-mustard mixture into the rim. Move the brisket with the tongs to the pan, fat-side up. Using a spatula to spread the sauce evenly, pour the rest of the BBQ sauce-mustard mixture over the top of the brisket. With aluminum foil, cover the pan tightly.

Return the brisket to the grill and continue to cook for 2 to 3 hours, or until the brisket is tender. The internal temperature should be 203 ° F on an instant-read meat thermometer.

Remove from the grill and allow the meat to rest at room temperature for between 15 and 20 minutes. Slice into 1/4 inch slices with a sharp knife through the grain and serve immediately. Enjoy! Enjoy!

Smoked Baked Potato Soup

SERVING	PREP TIME	COOK TIME	PELLETS
6	15 MINS	1 HOUR	APPLE

Skip the potato counter, mixing everything in every bite with this comforting soup.

INGREDIENTS:

6 Large russet potatoes
12 Ounce bacon
4 Tablespoon butter
1 Small onion, diced
1/4 Cup flour
4 Cup milk
1 Can chicken stock
1 Teaspoon onion powder
1 Teaspoon garlic powder
2 Teaspoon salt
1 Cup sour cream

DIRECTIONS:

Set the Traeger to 375 ° F when ready to cook, and preheat for 15 minutes, lid closed.

With a fork, poke the potatoes and put directly on the pan grill. 1 hour to cook. "Cook bacon for about 20 minutes on a baking sheet at the same time; remove, cool and cut into 1/2" bits.

Once the potatoes are done , remove them and allow 15 minutes to cool. Peel the potatoes carefully and cut them into 1-inch bits. Only set aside.

In a big dutch oven, heat the butter. Add the onion and sauté until translucent, 5-7 minutes, until it is melted and bubbly.

Before slowly adding the milk and chicken stock, add the flour to the butter and onion mixture and sauté for 1 minute, 1/2 cup at a time. Add the onion powder, garlic powder and 2 tsp salt when all the liquid is incorporated.

Drop the potato pieces in the soup and mash once incorporated, but still a little chunky, with a potato masher. Apply the sour cream and 3/4 of the bacon for garnish, reserving some.

Garnish with extra ingredients for the soup and serve soft.
Enjoy it.!.

Spicy Smoked Chili Beef Jerky

SERVING	PREP TIME	COOK TIME	PELLETS
5	8 HOURS	5 HOURS	HICKORY

Smoke this spicy jerky on the Traeger for a hot, hot, hot snack, then grab a bite whenever your fire is running low.

INGREDIENTS:

1 Cup chili sauce
1/3 Cup beer
2 Tablespoon soy sauce
1 Tablespoon Worcestershire sauce
1 Tablespoon curing salt
1 Tablespoon Pickled Jalapeno Peppers, minced
2 Pound flank steak

DIRECTIONS:

Combine the chili sauce, beer, soy sauce, Worcestershire sauce, salt, and pickled jalapeño peppers in a mixing bowl.

Put the beef slices in a large plastic bag that can be resealed. Pour the marinade mixture over the meat, then rub the bag so that the marinade covers all the slices. For several hours, or overnight, close the bag and refrigerate.

Set the temperature to 180 ° F when ready to cook and preheat for 15 minutes with the lid closed.

Remove the marinade from the beef; discard the marinade. Dry beef slices between towels made of paper. Arrange the meat directly on the grill grate or smoke shelf in a single layer.

Smoke for 4 to 5 hours, or while bending a slice, until the jerky is dry but still chewy and very pliant.

Transfer to a resealable plastic bag when it is still hot for the jerky. At room temperature, let the jerky rest for an hour. Squeeze some air from the bag and cool the jerky in the fridge. Pro Tip: for every cut of beef or wild game, you can use this recipe. Enjoy! Enjoy!

Smoked Ribs-Eyes with Bourbon Butter

SERVING	PREP TIME	COOK TIME	PELLETS
4	20 MINS	45 MINS	MESQUITE

Rib-eyes are, for good reason, the favorite steak of many discriminating meat eaters. These are taken to a whole new level by an hour's smoke accompanied by a fast sear and a luscious pat of bourbon flavored butter.

INGREDIENTS:

1/2 Cup butter, room temperature
2 Clove garlic, minced
2 Tablespoon bourbon
1 Tablespoon minced chives or green onions
1 Tablespoon minced parsley
1/2 Teaspoon salt
1/2 Teaspoon ground black pepper
4 (1 inch thick) rib-eye steaks
To Taste Traeger Prime Rib Rub

DIRECTIONS:

For the Bourbon Butter: In a small mixing bowl , add the butter, garlic, bourbon, chives, parsley, salt and pepper and stir with a wooden spoon. Butter can be prepared ahead and refrigerated until serving time.

When ready to cook, set the temperature of the Traeger to 180 ° F and preheat for 15 minutes, lid closed. If available, use Super Smoke for the optimal flavor.

Season the steaks generously with Traeger Prime Rib Rub.

Directly place the steaks on the grill grate and smoke for 1 hour.

Remove the steaks to a dish immediately and set the temperature of your Traeger to 500 ° F.

Return the steaks to the grill when the grill is hot, turning once, until they reach an internal temperature of 135 ° F for medium-rare, around 6 to 8 minutes on each side.

Move the steaks to a dish and cover each one immediately with a pat of bourbon butter.

Until serving, let the meat rest for 3 minutes. Enjoy Enjoy!

Smoked Venison Soft Tacos

SERVING	PREP TIME	COOK TIME	PELLETS
2	15 MINS	30 MINS	BIG GAME BLEND

Tucked into a soft tortilla, field-to-table freshness is garnished with a little green spice.

INGREDIENTS:

1 Pound Venison, back strap steaks
2 Tablespoon Traeger Big Game Rub
1/2 Pound Tomatillos
1 Medium jalapeño
2 Clove garlic
1 Medium yellow onion
3 Chiles, Anaheim
2 Whole limes
1/2 Cup cilantro, finely chopped
To Taste salt
4 flour tortillas
1 Whole avocados
1/4 Cup Queso fresco, crumbled
1/4 Cup cilantro leaves

DIRECTIONS:

Season with Traeger Big Game Rub for the steaks and set aside for 20 minutes at room temperature.

Start the Traeger when it is ready to cook and set the temperature to 185F and preheat for 10-15 minutes.

Directly put the steaks on the grill grill and cook for 30 to 45 minutes at 185F or until the internal temperature reaches 110 degrees F.

Roast the tomatillos, jalapeños, garlic , onion and chiles in the oven until lightly browned while the steaks are cooking. Move to a blender with roasted salsa verde ingredients and add lime juice, chopped coriander and salt to taste. Purée until it's smooth. Set aside until the tacos are ready to be built.

Remove from the grill when the steaks' internal temperature exceeds 110 degrees F. Boost the temperature of the grill to 500F and preheat it for 10 to 15 minutes, with the lid closed.

Place the steaks back on the grill at the temperature of the grill and sear for 2-4 minutes on each side or until the internal temperature reaches 130 degrees F for medium rareTake the steaks off the grill. When taken off the grill, they can continue to cook and should attain a final internal temperature of 135 degrees F. Take 10 minutes to rest before slicing.

Heat the tortillas, top with sliced venison, salsa verde, cheese fresco, and sliced avocado to serve and cilantro leaves. Enjoy! Enjoy!

Smoked Porterhouse Steak

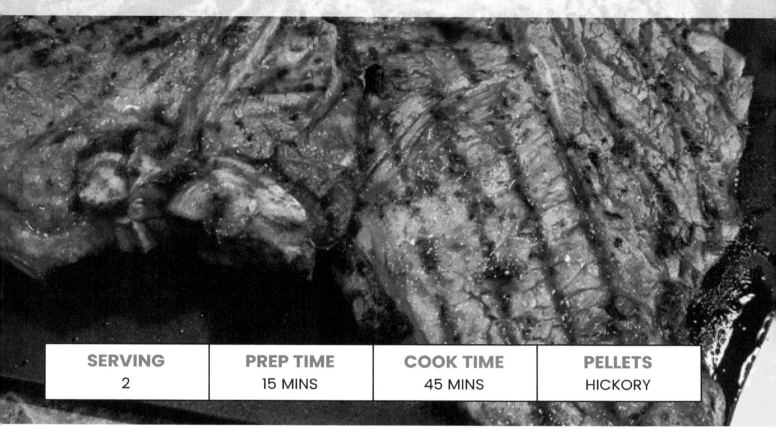

SERVING	PREP TIME	COOK TIME	PELLETS
2	15 MINS	45 MINS	HICKORY

Give your next steak dinner some big flavor. A melted butter, Worcestershire, and Dijon mix is brushed with thick porterhouse steaks, rubbed with our Coffee Rub, then smoked and seared to juicy perfection.

INGREDIENTS:

4 Tablespoon butter, melted
2 Tablespoon Worcestershire sauce
2 Teaspoon Dijon mustard
1 Teaspoon Traeger Coffee Rub
40 Ounce Steak, porterhouse

DIRECTIONS:

When ready to cook, set the temperature of the grill to 180 ° F and preheat for 15 minutes, lid closed. If available, use Super Smoke for the optimal flavor.

Combine the butter, mustard and Worcestershire sauce and whisk until smooth. Brush the steaks on both sides with the mixture. With Traeger Coffee Rub, season both sides of steak.

Put the steaks on the grill and smoke for 30 minutes. Using tongs to pass the steaks to a plate.

Increase the temperature and preheat to high. Set to 500 ° F for optimal results, if available. Brush the steaks with the butter-Worcestershire combination once again.

Return the steaks to the grill grill and cook to the perfect doneness when the grill comes to temperature. Cook at an internal temperature of 135 ° F for medium-well for medium rare, add several more minutes on each side. Let the steaks rest before serving for 5 minutes. Enjoy Enjoy!

Texas-Style Smoked Beef Brisket

INGREDIENTS:

1 (12-15 lb) brisket
2/3 Cup Butcher BBQ Prime Brisket Injection
2 Cup water
2 Tablespoon canola oil
1 1/2 Cup apple juice
1/2 Cup Traeger Prime Rib Rub
1/2 Cup Traeger Coffee Rub
2 Tablespoon ground black pepper
1/2 Cup Traeger Prime Rib Rub
1/2 Cup Traeger Coffee Rub
2 Tablespoon ground black pepper

SERVING	PREP TIME	COOK TIME	PELLETS
6	30 MINS	18 HOURS	TEXAS BEEF BLEND

This recipe for a brisket is worthy of any real Texan. Butchers Prime is injected into our full packer, sprayed with apple juice, coated with a combination of Traeger Prime Rib and Coffee Rub, topped with black pepper and smoked over oak wood.

DIRECTIONS:

Break off the top of the brisket 's fat cap and remove all the silverskin. Trim off any brown areas on the side of the brisket, for example. Make a long cut on the flat (thin side) of the brisket with the grain and a brief cut on the flat again to demonstrate the position of the cuts after cooking. Trim the thickness of the bottom fat cap to about 1/4 inch.

Combine an infusion of Butcher BBQ Prime Brisket and water. Injected in a checkerboard pattern into the brisket with the grain. Rub with canola oil on the whole brisket, then sprinkle with apple juice and let sit for 30 minutes.

Combine all Traeger rubs and brisket of the season liberally. Season with black pepper on top.

When ready to cook, set the temperature of the Traeger to 180 ° F and preheat for 15 minutes, lid closed. If available, use Super Smoke for the optimal flavor.

Place the brisket directly on the grill and cook the fat side down for 8 to 12 hours. After the first 3 hours, spritz the apple juice every 30 to 45 minutes.

Start taking the temperature after 8 hours by inserting about two thirds of the way up into the thickest section. About 150 ° F and 160 ° F, it should record. Once 160 ° F has been registered by the brisket, wrap two sheets of aluminum foil, leaving one end open. Pour in the remaining injection of brisket and close the foil package. On the grill, raise the temperature to 225 ° F and put the wrapped brisket directly on the grill. Cook until the internal temperature registers 204 ° F for another 3 to 4 hours.

Remove from the grill and put to rest for at least 2 hours in a cooler wrapped in a towel. Cut slices around the thickness of a pencil against the grain when ready to serve. Separate the cooking liquid from the fat if desired and pour the juices over the cut brisket slices. Enjoy! Enjoy!

Smoked Bologna

SERVING	PREP TIME	COOK TIME	PELLETS
4	5 MINS	4 HOURS	MESQUITE

Bologna is not just for sack lunches — it tastes fantastic stacked high on your favorite bun with rich, smoky flavor & toasted edges.

INGREDIENTS:

1 Pound bologna log
1/4 Cup brown sugar
1 Tablespoon yellow mustard
1 Teaspoon soy sauce
Dash Worcestershire sauce

DIRECTIONS:

Be careful not to cut too deep, score the bologna file.
Mix together the brown sugar, mustard, soy and Worcestershire sauce.
Rub it all over the bologna until mixed.
When ready to cook, set the temperature of the Traeger to 225 ° F and preheat for 15 minutes, lid closed.
For 3 to 4 hours, smoke bologna.
Remove and let cool from the grill.
Cut with the sandwiches and serve. Enjoy! Enjoy!

Tri-Tip Roast

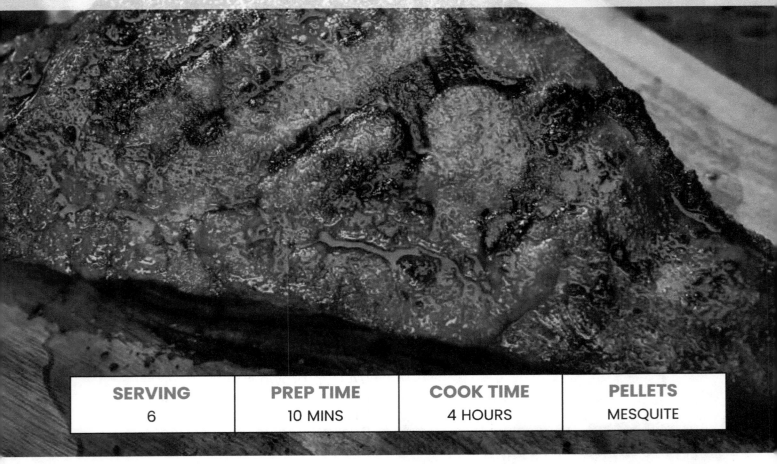

SERVING	PREP TIME	COOK TIME	PELLETS
6	10 MINS	4 HOURS	MESQUITE

Your status as Grill Master is assured by a well-seasoned tri-tip roast, barbecued to tender juiciness. Marinate your slab in Traeger BBQ Sauce, then shower it down the block with Traeger Prime Rib Rub for a competitive 'worthy' cue that will have your neighbors haulin'.

INGREDIENTS:

1 tri-tip roast
As Needed Traeger 'Que BBQ Sauce
As Needed Traeger Prime Rib Rub
1/2 Cup beef broth

DIRECTIONS:

Prep ahead. Marinate this recipe overnight. Marinate the tri-tip in the refrigerator overnight with Traeger 'Que BBQ Sauce.

Remove the tri-tip and discard the marinade. The Traeger Prime Rib Rub Light Season.

When ready to cook, set the temperature of the Traeger to 180 ° F and preheat for 15 minutes, lid closed.

Place the tri-tip for 3 to 4 hours on the grill and smoke.

Remove the tri-tip from the grill and put in 1/2 cup of beef broth with aluminum foil. Cover the aluminum foil and lift the temperature of the grill to 350 ° F.

Return the meat to the grill for 45 minutes. Remove from the grill and leave to rest before slicing for 15 minutes. Enjoy! Enjoy!

Smoked Paleo Beef Jerky

SERVING	PREP TIME	COOK TIME	PELLETS
6	8 HOURS	5 HOURS	MAPLE

With a little wood-fired protein boost, power through the day. For the ideal daily snack, Flank Steak is marinated in some savory spice and smoked over sweet maple wood.

INGREDIENTS:

1/2 Cup Tamari Sauce
1/4 Cup Worcestershire sauce
1 Tablespoon onion powder
1 Tablespoon garlic powder
1 Teaspoon black pepper
1/2 Teaspoon cayenne pepper
2 1/2 Pound flank steak

DIRECTIONS:

Combine the tamari sauce, Worcestershire sauce, garlic powder , onion powder, cayenne and black pepper in a mixing bowl. Stir to blend.
Trim from meat all connective tissue and extra fat. Slice it into 1/4 inch thick slices against the grain with a sharp knife. Put the slices in a big plastic bag that can be resealed.
Pour the mixture of the marinade over the beef, and rub the bag so that the marinade covers all the slices. For several hours, or overnight, close the bag and refrigerate.
Set the temperature to 180 ° F when ready to cook and preheat for 15 minutes with the lid closed.
Remove the beef and discard the marinade from the marinade. Arrange the meat directly on the grill grate in a single layer. Smoke for 4 to 5 hours, or when you bend a slice, until the jerky is dry but still chewy and very pliant.
Transfer to the refrigeration rack and allow for 1 hour to cool. Seal the leftover jerky in a plastic zip top bag and store it in the refrigerator. Enjoy Enjoy!

Simple Smoked Ribs

SERVING	PREP TIME	COOK TIME	PELLETS
6	15 MINS	8 HOURS	MAPLE

Use Traeger's Basic Smoked Ribs recipe to ease cooking ribs. Start with smoking baby backs on your Super Smoke or Smoke environment for 4 to 5 hours. Then wrap the rack in foil and smother it in BBQ sauce — that's all you need to do to perfect your fall-off-the-bone.

INGREDIENTS:

3 Rack baby back ribs
3/4 Cup Traeger Pork & Poultry Rub
3/4 Cup Traeger 'Que BBQ Sauce

DIRECTIONS:

Peel the membrane and trim any extra fat from the back of the ribs.

Season with Traeger Pork & Poultry Rub on both sides of the ribs, around 1/4 of a cup per rack.

When ready to cook, set the temperature of the Traeger to 180 ° F and preheat for 15 minutes, lid closed.

Place the ribs for 3 to 4 hours on the grill and smoke.

If the internal temperature is about 160 ° F-165 ° F, remove the ribs from the grill and lift the temperature of the grill to 350 ° F.

On a large sheet of heavy-duty aluminum foil, put around 1/4 cup of Traeger' Que BBQ Sauce, then place a rack of ribs meat side down on top and wrap tightly. For each rack, repeat.

Back on the grill, position the wrapped ribs and cook for 45 minutes or until the internal temperature is 204 ° F.

Remove from the grill and leave to rest before slicing for 20 minutes. Enjoy! Enjoy!

BBQ Brisket with Traeger Coffee Rub

SERVING	PREP TIME	COOK TIME	PELLETS
8	15 MINS	9 HOURS	HICKORY

Make the bark dark — beef is written all over it with our coffee rub. For a richness of taste that is absolutely unparalleled, this brisket is generously injected and seasoned with our fresh rub mixture.

INGREDIENTS:

15 Pound whole packer brisket
2 Tablespoon Traeger Coffee Rub
1 Cup water
2 Tablespoon salt
1/2 Cup water

DIRECTIONS:

Trim the excess fat off the brisket, leaving the bottom with a 1/4 inch tip.

In a small bowl, add 2 tbsp of coffee rub, 1 cup of water, and 2 tbsp of salt until most of the salt is dissolved. Inject the brisket with the coffee rub mixture every square inch or so. Season the remaining rub and remaining salt on the outside of the brisket.

Set the Traeger to 250 ° F when ready to cook and preheat, with the lid closed for 15 minutes.

Directly put the brisket on the grill grill and cook for around 6 hours or until the inside temperature reaches 160 ° F.

Two layers of foil cover the brisket and pour in 1/2 cup of water. Tightly seal the tin foil to contain the liquid. Raise the temperature to 275 ° F and return to the grill. Cook for an additional 3 hours or until the inner temperature reaches 204 ° F.

Remove and slice the brisket from the grill. Enjoy!

Smoked Brisket Marinade

SERVING	PREP TIME	COOK TIME	PELLETS
8	15 MINS	45 MINS	APPLE

Start right off with your full packer. From start to finish, this marinade mixes rich red wine, fresh garlic, mustard and Traeger Beef Rub for a smokin' flavor infusion.

INGREDIENTS:

4 Head bulb garlic
2 Cup red wine
1 Cup spicy brown mustard
1/2 Cup Agave Nectar
1/4 Cup extra-virgin olive oil
2 Tablespoon Traeger Beef Rub

DIRECTIONS:

To reveal the tops of the cloves, cut off the top of the garlic bulb. Drizzle the top with 1 teaspoon of olive oil.

Set the temperature to 180 ° F when ready to cook and preheat for 15 minutes with the lid closed. If available, use Super Smoke for the optimal flavor.

On the smoke setting, put garlic on the Traeger and roast for 30 to 45 minutes or until the cloves are tender. Remove and allow to cool from the grill.

Squeeze the garlic cloves into a tub and out of the bulb. Apply the remaining ingredients and combine until well blended.

In a large plastic bag, put the brisket and then apply the marinade. For no more than 2 hours per pound, marinate the brisket. During the marinade process, flip the brisket once. For directions, see our Smoked Brisket recipe when you're ready to cook brisket.

Smoked Tri Tip

SERVING	PREP TIME	COOK TIME	PELLETS
6	5 MINS	1 HOUR	PECAN

This tri-tip is everything a steak should be: juicy, tasty, and addicting, reverse-seared like a boss.

INGREDIENTS:

1 (3-5 lb) tri-tip
1/8 Cup pepper
1/8 Cup salt

DIRECTIONS:

When ready to cook, set the temperature of the Traeger to 225 ° F and preheat for 15 minutes, lid closed. If available, use Super Smoke for the optimal flavor.

Put salt and pepper together. With a thick coat of salt and pepper mixture, season all sides of the beef.

Place the tri-tip directly on the grill grill and cook it for around 60 to 90 minutes until it reaches an internal temperature of 130 ° F.

Take the grill off when the tri-tip exceeds 130 ° F and wrap it in foil.

Increase the temperature of the Traeger to 500 ° F and preheat it for 15 minutes with the lid closed.

When the grill reaches temperature, remove the tri-tip from the foil and sear on each side for 4 minutes.

Pull the grill off and allow 10 to 15 minutes to rest. Slice against the grain for serving. Enjoy! Enjoy!

Smoked Brisket

SERVING	PREP TIME	COOK TIME	PELLETS
8	15 MINS	9 HOURS	APPLE

We take everybody's favorite BBQ dish, brisket, and infuse it with our wood-fired signature taste. Forget seconds, on this mouthwatering whole packer, you'll be coming back for thirds.

INGREDIENTS:

2 Tablespoon garlic powder
2 Tablespoon onion powder
2 Tablespoon paprika
2 Teaspoon chile powder
1/3 Cup Jacobsen Salt or kosher salt
1/3 Cup coarse ground black pepper, divided
1 (12-14 lb) whole packer brisket, trimmed
1 1/2 Cup beef broth

DIRECTIONS:

When ready to cook, set the temperature of the Traeger to 225 ° F and preheat for 15 minutes, lid closed. If available, use Super Smoke for the optimal flavor.

For the Rub: In a small bowl , combine the garlic powder, onion powder, paprika, chili pepper, kosher salt and pepper. With the rub, season the brisket on all sides.

Place the brisket on the grill rack, fat side down. Cook the brisket for 5 to 6 hours, until it reaches an internal temperature of 160 ° F. Remove from the grill when the brisket reaches an internal temperature of 160 F.

Double seal the aluminum foil with the meat and apply the beef broth to the foil package. Return the brisket to the grill and cook for around 3 hours until it reaches an internal temperature of 204 ° F.

Remove from the grill once done, unwrap from the foil and let rest for 15 minutes. Slice the grain against it and serve.

58

Chefs Brisket

SERVING	PREP TIME	COOK TIME	PELLETS
8	10 MINS	8 HOURS	HICKORY

This brisket can't be messed up — we've built a bulletproof recipe & process for smoking the perfect brisket. Fire it up on a Friday night and feast like a king over the weekend.

INGREDIENTS:

1 (12 lb) whole packer beef brisket, fat trimmed to 1/4 inch
1/3 Cup Jacobsen Salt Co. Pure Kosher Sea Salt
2 Tablespoon garlic paste
2 Tablespoon onion powder
1/3 Cup black pepper

DIRECTIONS:

The day prior to cooking, season the brisket. In a small cup, combine the salt, garlic, onion powder and pepper together. Liberally season the beef. Place it overnight or for at least 8 hours in the refrigerator.

When ready to cook, set the temperature of the Traeger to 225 ° F and preheat for 15 minutes, lid closed. If available, use Super Smoke for the optimal flavor.

Place the brisket, fat side down, right in the middle of the grill on the grill grate. For around 4 to 5 hours, or until the brisket reaches an internal temperature of 160 ° F to 165 ° F, smoke the brisket.

Take the grill out of the brisket and wrap it in butcher paper or foil. Continue to smoke at 225 ° F until the brisket reaches an internal temperature of 203 ° F, around another 3 to 4 hours, for a total of 8 to 10 hours of cooking and smoking period.

Remove butcher paper or brisket wrapped with foil from the grill and allow one hour to rest.

Slice the brisket into 1/4 inch thick slices against the grain after resting, and serve.

Smoked Lamb Sousage

SERVING	PREP TIME	COOK TIME	PELLETS
6	2 HOURS	1 HOUR	CHERRY

This smoked lamb sausage is a simple and tasty introduction to the development of sausages, and it is very good for Traegers.

INGREDIENTS:

Units of Measurement:
2 Pound lamb shoulders
1 Tablespoon garlic, minced
1 Teaspoon cumin
1 Teaspoon paprika
1/2 Teaspoon cayenne pepper
2 Tablespoon Fennel, ground
1 Tablespoon cilantro, finely chopped
1 Tablespoon parsley, minced
1 Teaspoon black pepper
2 Tablespoon salt
1 Hog Casings
3 Cup Yogurt, Greek
1 Whole lemon juice
1 Clove garlic
1 Whole Cucumber, peeled
1 Tablespoon Dill, fresh or dried
To Taste salt
To Taste black pepper

DIRECTIONS:

Break the lamb shoulder into 2 " pieces, and using a meat grinder, grind the meat.

Lightly mix the lamb with all the spices in a bowl and refrigerate. To give the sausage a good texture, it is important to refrigerate the ground lamb so that the fat does not melt.

Then, attach the hog casing (60 inch) using a sausage horn and begin to feed the sausage back through the grinder to fill the casing and twist into ties.

Prick holes all over the casing with a paring knife (this will allow steam to escape while cooking). Only refrigerate.

Combine all of the yogurt sauce ingredients in a medium-sized dish. Cover and hold refrigerated.

Set the Traeger to 225 º F when ready to cook and preheat with the lid closed for 15 minutes.

On the grill grate, put the prepared sausage and smoke it for 1 hour.

Remove the links from the grill once the hour is over and crank the grill up to 500F and preheat.

Place the links back on the grill when the grill reaches temperature and cook on each side for 5 minutes.

Serve it hot on the side with yogurt sauce and roasted potatoes. Enjoy Enjoy!

Cowgirl Cut Smoked Steak

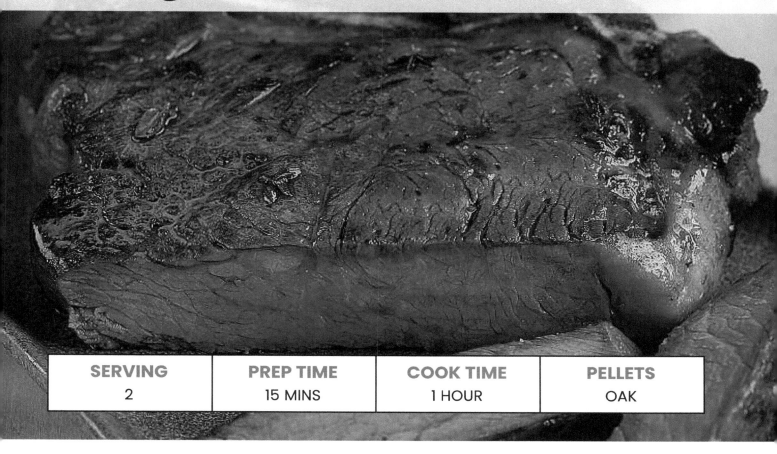

SERVING	PREP TIME	COOK TIME	PELLETS
2	15 MINS	1 HOUR	OAK

Before getting smoked and reverse-seared to perfection, this cowgirl cut steak recipe from Lydia Mondavi begins with our Napa Valley influenced rub with red wine, fennel and garlic notes. Substitute any rub of your choosing, but we highly recommend trying out Rob & Lydia Mondavi's limited Winemakers Rub for ultimate flavor.

INGREDIENTS:

1 New York or Rib Eye Steak, 1" or more
As Needed Traeger Winemaker's Napa Valley Rub

DIRECTIONS:

Set the temperature to 180 ° F when ready to cook and preheat for 15 minutes with the lid closed. If available, use Super Smoke for the optimal flavor.

With Traeger Winemaker's Rub, season all sides of the steak generously.

Put the steak on the barbecue grill and smoke for 60 minutes. Take it off the grill and set it aside to rest.

Increase the temperature and preheat to 500 ° F, with the lid closed.

Place the steak back on the grill grate when the grill is hot. For medium rare, sear until steaks hit the ideal internal temperature, 125-130 ° F.

Serve with rich, bold red wine or delicious rocks of bourbon. Enjoy! Enjoy!

Grilled Molasses and Chili Tri-Tip

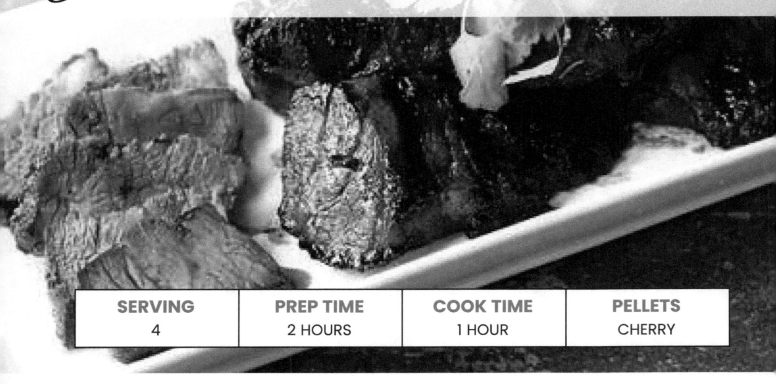

SERVING	PREP TIME	COOK TIME	PELLETS
4	2 HOURS	1 HOUR	CHERRY

With Traeger's molasses and chili marinade recipe, try a fresh take on tri-tip. Simply marinate the tri-tip for up to two hours before bumping up the heat to high and pulling the meat once it reaches 130 ° F. Smoke for an hour.

INGREDIENTS:

1/4 Cup brown sugar
1/4 Cup molasses
3 Tablespoon soy sauce
2 Tablespoon rice vinegar
1 Tablespoon extra-virgin olive oil
5 Clove garlic
2 Teaspoon chili powder
1 Teaspoon ginger, minced
1/2 Teaspoon black pepper
2 Pound tri-tip
2 Tablespoon water

DIRECTIONS:

Combine the brown sugar, molasses, soy sauce, rice vinegar, olive oil, garlic (crushed and peeled), chili powder, ginger, and black pepper in a large glass bowl or cup. Whisk in order to blend. Place the tri-tip and transform to coat in the marinade. Marinate, wrapped, for 1 to 2 hours, turning halfway through the steak.

Set the temperature to 180 ° F when ready to cook and preheat for 15 minutes with the lid closed. If available, use Super Smoke for the optimal flavor.

Place the steak on the grill grate directly and smoke for 1 hour. Do not throw the marinade away.

Remove the tri-tip from the grill and turn the grill up to high and preheat for 15 minutes with the lid closed. Set to 500 ° F for optimal results, if available.

Back in the marinade, position the tri-tip and coat it on both sides. Put the steak back on the grill and cook, turning once, around 5-8 minutes on each side, until the internal temperature reaches 135 ° F. Remove the steak from the grill and leave to rest for 10-15 minutes, uncovered, before cutting.

Place the remaining marinade in a saucepan with 2 tablespoons of water while the steak rests and bring it to a boil. Reduce the heat and leave for 5 minutes to simmer. If needed, serve alongside the tri-tip. Enjoy! Enjoy!

Pork Recipes

FOR WOOD PELLET SMOKER GRILLS

Smoked Pork Chops with Ale-Balsamic Glaze

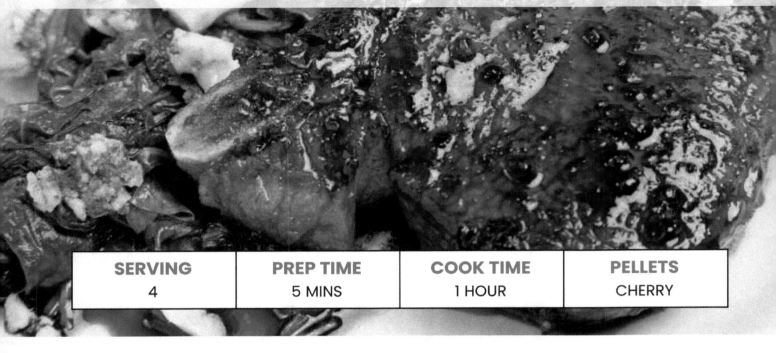

SERVING	PREP TIME	COOK TIME	PELLETS
4	5 MINS	1 HOUR	CHERRY

This balsamic glaze makes a sticky sweet chop that even kids can eat, whether you're using ginger ale or Pale Ale.

INGREDIENTS:

4 (8 oz) bone-in pork rib chops
As Needed Traeger Pork & Poultry Rub
67/100 Cup ginger ale or pale ale beer
1/4 Cup brown sugar
1/2 Cup balsamic vinegar
2 Sprig rosemary, leaves finely chopped
As Needed olive oil

DIRECTIONS:

Set Traeger temperature to 165 ° F when ready to cook and preheat for 15 minutes, lid closed. Use Super Smoke for the optimal flavor if available.

Season the pork rib chops with Traeger Pork & Poultry Rub on all sides, gently pressing the seasoning into the meat.

On the grill grill, place the pork rib chops and leave to smoke for 30 minutes.

Make the glaze meanwhile. On medium-low heat, reduce the ginger ale, brown sugar, balsamic vinegar and chopped rosemary leaves on the stovetop until it thickens to the point that the back of a spoon can be coated but still pourable (about 15 to 20 minutes). While the pork rib chops finish smoking, maintain the glaze warm.

Remove the pork rib chops and lift the temperature of the Traeger to 500 ° F and preheat for 15 minutes with the lid closed.

Lightly drizzle the olive oil on the pork rib chops and place them back on the grill grill and cook for 5 minutes.

Flip and baste the pork rib chops with the glaze. Cook on an instant-read thermometer for 5 more minutes or until the internal temperatures reach 145 ° F. Remove from the Traeger, leave to rest before slicing for 10 minutes. Enjoy Enjoy!

Smoked Pork Tenderloin

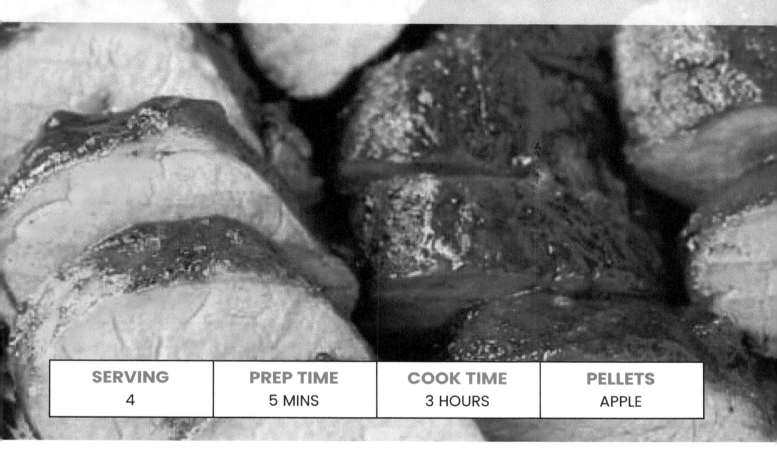

SERVING	PREP TIME	COOK TIME	PELLETS
4	5 MINS	3 HOURS	APPLE

Give a sweet and smoky kick to your pork. These tenderloins are marinated and perfectly smoked over aromatic applewood pellets in a sweet honey and thyme mixture.

INGREDIENTS:

1/2 Cup apple juice
3 Tablespoon honey
3 Tablespoon Traeger Pork & Poultry Rub
1/4 Cup brown sugar
2 Tablespoon thyme leaves
1/2 Tablespoon black pepper
2 (1-1/2 lb) pork tenderloins, silverskin removed

DIRECTIONS:

Add the apple juice, honey (warm), Traeger Pork & Poultry rub, brown sugar, thyme leaves and black pepper to the marinade in a large bowl. Whisk in order to combine.
Add pork loins to the bowl with the marinade. Turn pork to coat and cover bowl with plastic wrap.
Transfer to the refrigerator and leave for 2 to 3 hours to marinate.
When ready to cook, set the temperature of the Traeger to 225 ° F and preheat for 15 minutes, lid closed. If available, use Super Smoke for the optimal flavor.
Place the tenderloins directly on the grill and smoke until 145 ° F, around 2-1/2 to 3 hours, is registered in the inner temperature.
Remove from grill and let rest 5 minutes before slicing. Enjoy! Enjoy!

Bacon Old-Fashioned Cocktail

SERVING	PREP TIME	COOK TIME	PELLETS
2	5 MINS	20 MINS	APPLE

A "Old-Fashioned" take on the classic timeless. You'll never go back to the old style, Bourbon supported and bacon-infused.

INGREDIENTS:

8 Slices bacon
1/4 Cup warm water (110°F to 115°F)
750 mL bourbon
1/4 Fluid Ounce maple syrup
2 Dash Angostura bitters
1 fresh orange peel

DIRECTIONS:

Smoke bacon using this recipe for Applewood Smoked Bacon prior to making Old Fashioned.

To make bacon: Set the Traeger to 325 ° F when ready to cook and preheat for 15 minutes, lid closed.

Put bacon in a single layer on a cooling rack that fits within a baking sheet pan. Cook for 15-20 minutes or until the bacon is browned and crispy in Traeger. For later, save bacon. Let the fat cool slightly; to infuse the bourbon, you can use the fat.

In a glass or large plastic tub, mix 1/4 cup of warm (not hot) liquid bacon fat with the entire contents of a 750ml bottle of bourbon.

To stir well, use a fork. Let it sit for a few hours on the table, stirring every so often.

Put the bourbon fat mixture in the freezer for about four hours. The fat will congeal after approximately an hour and you can easily scoop it out with a spoon. If needed, you can fine-strain the blend through a sieve to extract all the fat.

Use ice to combine ingredients and stir until cold. Strain in an Old Fashioned glass over fresh ice and garnish with the reserved bacon and orange peel. Enjoy! Enjoy!

Smothered Pork Chops

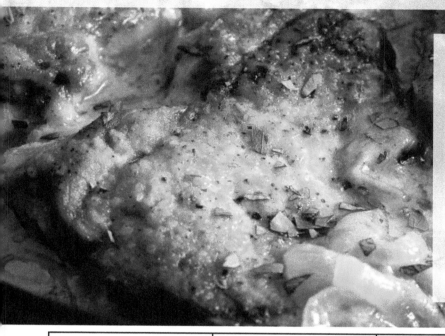

INGREDIENTS:

1/2 Cup all-purpose flour
1/4 Cup Cornmeal
2 Teaspoon kosher salt
1 1/2 Teaspoon ground black pepper
1/2 Cup whole milk
1 Large egg yolk
1 1/2 Cup peanut or canola oil
4 Whole (6-8 oz) bone-in single-cut pork chops

SERVING	PREP TIME	COOK TIME	PELLETS
4	20 MINS	30 MINS	APPLE

For a saucy bite, smother your chops. Fried pork chops and smothered in scratch-made gravy for an enticingly simple meal, baked to wood-fired perfection.

DIRECTIONS:

Start the Traeger grill at a set temperature of 250 degrees F when ready to cook, and preheat, lid closed, for 10 to 15 minutes.

Whisk the rice, cornmeal, salt and pepper together. On a tray, position the mixture.

Add milk and egg yolk in a medium sized dish. Whisk in order to blend.

Pour the oil into a pan of cast iron on the stove and heat the oil on a frying thermometer to 375 degrees F. Switch down the heat to medium-high heat.

Submerge the pork chops with the eggs and milk in the tub, then press the pork chops into the flour mixture pan, turn and repeat on the other side. Shake off some superfluous flour.

Slide in the hot oil with the pork chops. Fry until both sides are completely golden brown. Around two minutes on each hand.

Move the pork chops to a baking tray and let the grill finish cooking. An internal temperature of 145 degrees F. should be achieved by chops.

To make the gravy: Pour out all the cast iron oil, except 1 Tbsp. In the cast iron skillet, add the onion and cook until translucent but not browned, about 4 minutes, stirring. In the pan, sprinkle the flour and cook , stirring for approximately 3 minutes, until the flour is uniformly dispersed throughout the onion and toasted.

Add milk and broth, and whisk until smooth. Bring to a boil and simmer, stirring for about 2 minutes, until the gravy has reached the desired thickness. Season with salt and pepper to taste.

Remove the chops from the grill and put them on a serving plate. With the sauce, smother them and eat. Enjoy! Enjoy!

BBQ Rib Sandwich

SERVING	PREP TIME	COOK TIME	PELLETS
2	15 MINS	3 HOURS	HICKORY

One bite of this super-sized sandwich, and you're going to be transported to the sky of ribs. Our take on the famous classic of fast food is packed with the flavor of Traeger hickory and large enough to share.

INGREDIENTS:

3 Rack baby back pork ribs
As Needed cracked black pepper
As Needed kosher salt
1/2 Cup Traeger 'Que BBQ Sauce
4 hoagie rolls
1/2 Cup Traeger 'Que BBQ Sauce
1 Jar Pickles
1 yellow onion, thinly sliced

DIRECTIONS:

The peeling membrane on the back of the ribs. With crushed black pepper and salt, season lightly.

Set the Traeger to 225 ° F when ready to cook and preheat with the lid closed for 15 minutes.

Cook for two hours on the meaty side, then flip down the ribs on the meaty side and cook for another hour.

Remove the ribs from the grill and turn over so that on a cutting board they lie bone side up. Cut down the middle of each bone using a sharp knife and use your fingertips to extract the bones.

With half of the Traeger 'Que BBQ Sauce, turn the ribs back over and brush. Put the sauce back on the grill for 5-10 minutes. Remove and set aside from the barbecue.

To fit the length of the hoagie rolls, cut rib racks. Break the hoagie rolls in half and put the bottom bun on the ribs.

Top with onions, pickles, more BBQ sauce and top bun. Enjoy! Enjoy!

Smoked Pork Loin with Sauerkraut and Apples

SERVING	PREP TIME	COOK TIME	PELLETS
4	15 MINS	2 HOURS	APPLE

Pennsylvanian pork is epicly braised in a delicious sweet , sour, and beer medley.

INGREDIENTS:

2 1/2 Pound Pork, Loins
As Needed Sweet rub
1 Pound Sauerkraut
2 Granny Smith Apples, Peeled and Diced
1 sweet onion, thinly sliced
1/3 Cup brown sugar
1 Cup dark beer
2 Tablespoon butter
2 Bay Leaf

DIRECTIONS:

When ready to cook, set the temperature of the grill to 180 ° F and preheat for 15 minutes, lid closed.

With Traeger Sweet Rub, or salt and pepper, season the pork loin on all sides. Directly place the roast on the pan grill, close the lid and smoke for 1 hour.

Layer the sauerkraut, apples, onions, brown sugar, beer, butter, and bay leaves in a large Dutch oven or glass baking dish. Lay the loin of smoked pork directly on top of the mixture of sauerkraut. With a cover or a sheet of foil, top the pan.

Turn the grill temperature up to 350 ° F and place the pan back on the grill. Close the lid and roast the pork for an extra hour or until the internal temperature reads 160 ° F on an instant-read meat thermometer.

To a cutting board, move the roast and let it rest. Meanwhile, swirl the sauerkraut mixture gently and place it on a serving plate. Slice and layer the pork roast on the sauerkraut and apples. Enjoy! Enjoy!.

Smoked Pork Loin

SERVING	PREP TIME	COOK TIME	PELLETS
6	5 MINS	3 HOURS	CHERRY

A tasty cut from the back of the hog is pork loin. Forget about the supermarket, it's filled with preservatives. Grab the butcher 's new, tender slab so you can rub it down with the most savory of our Traeger rubs.

INGREDIENTS:

1 Pork, Loins
As Needed Traeger Rub

DIRECTIONS:

Pork loin with Traeger Rub for the season.
When ready to cook, set the temperature of the grill to 180 ° F and preheat for 15 minutes, lid closed.
Place the pork loin, diagonally, on the grill grates, and smoke for 3 to 4 hours.
Increase the temperature of the grill to 350 ° F and bake for 20 to 30 minutes.
"Cut into 1-1/2" steaks and remove from the grill. Eat. Enjoy!

Smoked Classic Porchetta

SERVING	PREP TIME	COOK TIME	PELLETS
8	8 HOURS	3 HOURS	APPLE

Build this crisp, salty, delicious Italian classic with our recipe for Smoked Porchetta.

INGREDIENTS:

4 Clove garlic, minced
2 Tablespoon rosemary, chopped
2 Teaspoon salt
1 Teaspoon black pepper
1 Teaspoon red pepper flakes
6 Pound Pork Belly, skin on
To Taste salt
To Taste black pepper
3 Pound Pork Loin, boneless, center cut
To Taste salt
To Taste black pepper
To Taste salt
To Taste black pepper

DIRECTIONS:

For the garlic mixture: Combine the minced garlic, rosemary, salt, pepper and red pepper flakes in a medium cup.

On a clean work surface, put belly skin side up and score skin in a crosshatch pattern. Flip the stomach over and season the side of the flesh with salt and pepper and half the garlic mixture.

In the middle of the belly, put the trimmed pork loin and rub with the remaining garlic mixture and season with salt and pepper to taste.

To form a cylindrical shape, roll the pork belly around the loin and tie tightly with kitchen twine at intervals of 1'. Season with salt and pepper on the skin and move to the refrigerator, uncovered, and overnight let air dry.

Set the temperature to 180 ° F when ready to cook and preheat for 15 minutes with the lid closed.

Directly put the porchetta seam side down on the grill grille and smoke for 1 hour.

Increase the grill temperature to 325 ° F after an hour and roast until the inner temperature reaches 135 ° F, for around 2-1/2 hours. Tent with foil if the outside starts to burn before the target inner temperature is reached.

Remove from the grill and let stand before slicing for 30 minutes. Enjoy! Enjoy!

Smoked Traeger Pulled Pork

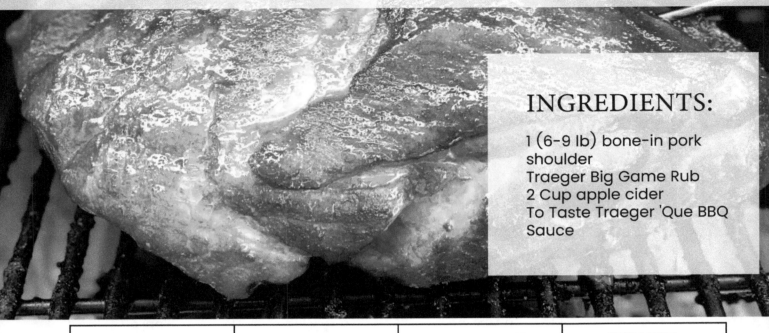

INGREDIENTS:

1 (6-9 lb) bone-in pork shoulder
Traeger Big Game Rub
2 Cup apple cider
To Taste Traeger 'Que BBQ Sauce

SERVING	PREP TIME	COOK TIME	PELLETS
8	10 MINS	9 HOURS	APPLE

Low-smoke it, slow-smoke it. Great pulled pork is worth the wait, and it is possible to serve this versatile BBQ meat any way you want.

DIRECTIONS:

Set the Traeger temperature to 250 ° F when ready to cook and preheat, with the lid closed for 15 minutes.

Trim the excess fat off the pork butt while the Traeger reaches temperature.

Season generously with both sides of the Traeger Big Game Rub and let sit for 20 minutes.

Directly on the pan grill, put the pork butt fat side up and cook until the internal temperature reaches 160 ° F, around 3 to 5 hours.

From the grill, remove the pork butt.

Stack 4 large sheets of aluminum foil on top of each other on a large baking sheet, ensuring they are big enough to wrap the pork butt completely on all sides. If not, to build a broader base, overlap the foil bits. Place the pork butt on the foil in the middle, then bring the sides of the foil up to the top of the pork butt a little bit before pouring the apple cider. Tightly tie the foil around the bacon, promising that the cider does not escape.

Place the foil-wrapped pork butt back on the side of the grill fat and cook until the internal temperature reaches 204 ° F, around 3 to 4 hours longer depending on the size of the pork butt in the thickest part of the meat.

Delete it from your barbecue. Enable the pork in the foil packet to rest for 45 minutes.

Remove the pork from the foil and into a fat separator to pour off any excess liquid.

Place the pork in a large dish and shred the meat, with the bone and any excess fat removed and discarded. Return separated liquid to pork and season with additional Traeger Big Game Rub to taste. Add Traeger 'Que BBQ Sauce or your favorite BBQ sauce to taste as an option.

Serve on your own, with your favourite meals, or with sandwiches. Refrigerate the leftover pork for up to 4 days in a sealed bag. Enjoy! Enjoy!

Smoked Burgers

SERVING	PREP TIME	COOK TIME	PELLETS
8	15 MINS	2 HOURS	MESQUITE

Your weekend BBQ will be one for the books with this juicy burger.

INGREDIENTS:

2 Pound ground beef
1 Tablespoon Worcestershire sauce
2 Tablespoon Traeger Beef Rub

DIRECTIONS:

Combine ground beef with Traeger Beef rub and Worcestershire sauce.

Form the mixture of beef into 8 hamburger patties.

When ready to cook, set the temperature of the Traeger to 180 ° F and preheat for 15 minutes, lid closed. If available, use Super Smoke for the optimal flavor.

For 2 hours, put patties directly on the grill grill and smoke.

Remove from the grill after 2 hours and serve with your favourite toppings. Enjoy! Enjoy!

Smoked Sausage Pancake Sandwich

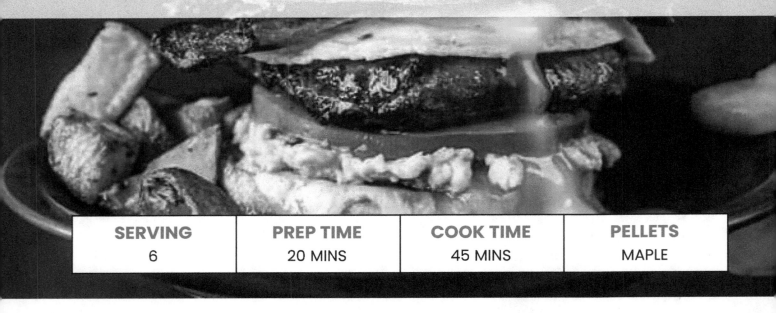

SERVING	PREP TIME	COOK TIME	PELLETS
6	20 MINS	45 MINS	MAPLE

Goodbye to dull, and goodbye to EPIC. For a breakfast fit for champions, smoked sausage is loaded and piled on top of homemade pancakes.

INGREDIENTS:

1 Pound ground pork
1 egg white
1/2 Teaspoon fresh thyme
1/2 Teaspoon Fennel, ground
1/2 Teaspoon onion powder
1 1/2 Teaspoon salt
1/4 Teaspoon ground nutmeg
1/2 Teaspoon Traeger Pork & Poultry Rub
2 Teaspoon maple syrup
1/2 Teaspoon black pepper
6 Cup whole wheat flour
1/2 Cup sugar
2 Tablespoon baking powder
1 Tablespoon baking soda
2 Teaspoon salt
5 Cup milk
1 Whole eggs
1 Tablespoon vegetable oil
2 Tablespoon maple syrup

DIRECTIONS:

In a tub, add all of the ingredients for the maple sausage and combine well. For 15 minutes, refrigerate.

When ready to cook, set the temperature of the grill to 180 ° F and preheat for 15 minutes, lid closed. If available, use Super Smoke for the optimal flavor.

Shape the mixture of pork into 8 round patties, grill and smoke for 30 minutes.

The smoked sausage patties are removed from the grill and set aside.

Turn the grill temperature to high and preheat for 15 minutes with the lid closed. Set to 500 ° F for optimal results, if available. As it preheats, put a big cast iron skillet or cast-iron griddle on the grill.

For the pancakes: Combine the dry ingredients for the pancakes in a large mixing bowl while the skillet preheats. To the dry ingredients, add the milk, egg, canola oil, and maple syrup and blend until mixed.

Place the preheated skillet with a few pads of butter and coat evenly. Apply 1/4 of a cup of the pancake mix to your skillet. At a time without overcrowding, fit as many as possible.

Close the lid and cook for 5 minutes or until the mixture bubbles. Flip and cook for another 2 to 3 minutes after bubbling once. Remove to cool on a tray.

For the smoked sausage: Put the smoked sausage patties directly on the grill and cook until golden brown or for 3 minutes per hand. With the bacon and pancakes, assemble your sandwiches. Connect the fried egg and cheese, if desired, to the sandwich. On top, place a pad of butter and drizzle with maple syrup. Enjoy! Enjoy!

Hawaiian Pulled Pig

SERVING	PREP TIME	COOK TIME	PELLETS
4	15 MINS	5 HOURS	HICKORY

This reconstruction of a typical centerpiece of luau is tropical & nice. Our little piggy is slowly roasted with smoke & wrapped in banana leaves for a dish that is truly a Hawaiian sky bite.

INGREDIENTS:

7 Pound bone-in pork shoulder
3 Tablespoon Jacobsen Salt Co. Pure Kosher Sea Salt
As Needed ground black pepper
2 Whole Banana Leaves

DIRECTIONS:

The pork shoulder is seasoned with Jacobsen salt and pepper.

On your work surface, put a banana leaf. In the middle of it, lie the pork shoulder and draw the ends up as if you were wrapping a present. At right angles to the first, lay the second banana leaf and draw up the ends to enclose the meat. Tightly wrap the whole box in aluminum foil. Overnight, refrigerate.

Set the Traeger to 300 degrees F when ready to cook and preheat with the lid closed for 15 minutes.

Place the wrapped pork directly on the grill and cook until the pork is tender, 5 to 6 hours, or until the internal temperature has reached 190 degrees F.

Switch the pork to a cutting board and leave to rest for 20 minutes, still wrapped. Unwrap the pork carefully and store any juices that have collected in the foil.

Tear the pork into bits and shreds, and remove any fat or bone lumps. Enjoy! Enjoy!

BBQ Pulled Pork and Pork Belly Banh Mi

SERVING	PREP TIME	COOK TIME	PELLETS
4	4 HOURS	11 HOURS	OAK

A wood-fired variation on a Bánh mì classic. This sandwich is filled with two forms of pork, doused with a homemade sauce, stuffed with a spicy mayo in a crusty baguette and topped with all the usual fixings.

INGREDIENTS:

4 Pound pork belly, skin removed
3333333333333333/10000000000000000 Cup salt
3333333333333333/10000000000000000 Cup brown sugar
1 Tablespoon black pepper
10 Pound Bone-In Pork Butt
1 Tablespoon salt
1 Cup apple juice
4 Tablespoon brown sugar
3 Tablespoon salt
1 Tablespoon black pepper
1/2 Cup apple juice
1 To Taste salt and black pepper
2 Tablespoon sesame oil
1/2 Cup onion, diced small
3 Clove garlic, minced
2 Tablespoon ginger, minced
3/4 Cup tomato sauce
2 Tablespoon soy sauce
2 Tablespoon water
3 Tablespoon rice vinegar
1/4 Cup Thai sweet chile sauce
3 Whole Carrots, cut into matchsticks
1 Whole Daikon, cut into matchsticks
2 Cup water
2 Tablespoon sugar
1 Tablespoon salt
2 Tablespoon rice vinegar
1 Cup mayonnaise
2 Tablespoon Sriracha
1 Whole lime, juiced
1 To Taste salt
1 Whole Baguette, enough for 8 sandwiches sliced lengthwise
1 Whole English Cucumber, thinly sliced lengthwise
2 Whole jalapeño, thinly sliced
1 Bunch cilantro leaves, picked

DIRECTIONS:

For the Pork Belly: Score in a crosshatch pattern (only 1/4 "deep) the fat on the pork belly. Combine the salt, brown sugar and black pepper, then rub all over the belly of the pork. Cover and put overnight in the refrigerator.

Set the grill temperature to high and preheat when ready to cook, the lid closed for 15 minutes. Directly put the pork belly on the grill grill and cook for 30 minutes.

Reduce the temperature to 275 degrees F and cook until a skewer inserted into the thickest portion easily slides in and out for an additional 2 hours.

For the Pulled Pork: Trim all excess fat from the pork butt, leaving 1/4 "of the fat cap attached. In a small bowl , mix 1 cup of apple juice, brown sugar and 1 tbsp of salt until most of the sugar and salt are dissolved.

Injecte the pork butt with the apple juice mixture per square inch or so. Season the pork butt exterior with the remaining salt and black pepper..

Set the Traeger to 250 ° F when ready to cook and preheat, with the lid closed for 15 minutes. Put the pork butt directly on the grill grate and cook for around 6 hours or until 160 ° F is reached indoors. Cover the pork butt and pour 1/2 cup of apple juice into two layers of foil. Tightly secure the tin foil in order to protect the apple juice.

In the case of leaks, increase the temperature to 275 ° F and return to the grill in a pan big enough to accommodate the pork butt. Cook for another 3 hours or until the internal temperature exceeds 205 degrees F.

Remove and discard the bone from the grill. Shred the pork with any extra fat or tendons removed. When required, season with additional salt and pepper.

For the Pulled Pork Sauce: Heat sesame oil over medium-high heat in a small saucepan. Add the onion and sauté for 1 to 2 minutes, until translucent. Add the garlic and ginger and sauté until fragrant, for 30 seconds. Add the tomato sauce, soy, water, chili sauce, and vinegar. Cook and then remove from the heat for 5 minutes. Pour the shredded pork over it and combine well. Reserve. Reserve.

For Pickled Vegetables: Add warm water, sugar , salt and rice vinegar to make the pickled vegetables, and mix until the sugar and salt dissolve. Pour the mixture over the matchstick vegetables, cover for at least 4 hours and refrigerate.

For the Sriracha Mayo: Add all the ingredients together and combine well. On each side of the sliced baguette, spread around 2 tablespoons of the mayo.

Line the sandwich with the cucumber, onion and jalapeños cut together. Top with sliced pork belly, pickled carrots, daikon and cilantro and fill with a portion of the pulled pork. Immediately serve. Enjoy, enjoy!

Lynchburg Bacon

SERVING	PREP TIME	COOK TIME	PELLETS
6	10 MINS	20 MINS	MAPLE

Bacon like you never had, soaked in the pride and joy of Tennessee, dredged in a sweet-savoury flour blend, and baked on a Traeger.

INGREDIENTS:

1 Pound Bacon, contry style
1 Cup whiskey
3/4 Cup flour
333/1000 Cup brown sugar
1 Teaspoon black pepper

DIRECTIONS:

Separate the slices of bacon and place them in a big, resealable plastic bag.
Stir the Traeger Sweet Rub into the whiskey if it is used. Pour the whiskey over the bacon to cover all the slices by massaging the bag. Put aside for 30 minutes at the very least.
Sift the flour, brown sugar, and black pepper together on a sheet of wax paper. Transfer to a second plastic bag that is resealable.
Drain the bacon and apply a few slices at a time to the flour mixture. Shake the bag to evenly cover each piece, then place it on the prepared baking pan in a single layer.
Start the Traeger grill, set the temperature to 375F, and preheat for 10 to 15 minutes with the lid closed.
Bake the bacon for about 20 to 25 minutes, until it is golden brown and crisp. Enjoy! Enjoy!

Bacon Weave Smoked Country Sausage

INGREDIENTS:

Pound Sausage, Uncooked
As Needed Traeger Pork &
Poultry Rub
8 Slices bacon

SERVING	PREP TIME	COOK TIME	PELLETS
4	15 MINS	2 HOURS	HICKORY

With bacon, everything's better and this dish is no exception. It looks amazing, but for family or friends, it's a breeze.

DIRECTIONS:

Shape the sausage into a loaf-shape using your hands. Using Traeger Pork and Poultry Shake, season lightly.

Set the temperature to 180 ° F when ready to cook and preheat for 15 minutes with the lid closed. For 1-1/2 hours, place the sausage loaf directly on the grill grate and smoke.

Assemble the bacon weave on a piece of wax paper while saucers are smoking. Next, set out 4 bacon pieces so that they meet each other on the wax paper. Next, lie the fifth piece of bacon so that the others are crossed. Under the 5th piece of bacon, tuck every other slice. Find the two bacon pieces that were under the fifth bacon piece and fold them back on top of themselves.

Put down the sixth bacon piece and unfold the two bits that have been laid back. Continue to fold the bacon back, two pieces at a time, laying the next piece of bacon on top until the weave is complete, which was most recently under the last piece of bacon. Only set aside. Take it off the grill after your sausage has smoked for 1-1/2 hours and raise the heat of your Traeger, close the lid to 350 ° F and preheat.

Wrap your sausage loaf in the bacon weave while your grill is heating up. Directly put the core of the weave on top of the sausage loaf and press the bacon all around the sausage.

To complete the weaving on the bottom of the sausage, turn the sausage and bacon over. The bacon ends alternate around the bottom and tuck the ends around each other.

Return your sausage to the grill and cook for 25-30 minutes until the sausage's internal temperature reaches 160 ° F. Enjoy! Enjoy!

Bacon Stuffed Smoked Pork Loin

SERVING	PREP TIME	COOK TIME	PELLETS
4	20 MINS	1 HOUR	PECAN

Try this deliciously tender walnut & craisin stuffed pork loin if you're crazy for bacon.

INGREDIENTS:

3 Pound Pork Loin, Butterflied
As Needed Traeger Pork &
Poultry Rub
1/4 Cup Walnuts, Chopped
1/3 Cup Craisins
1 Tablespoon fresh oregano
1 Tablespoon fresh thyme
6 Pieces asparagus, ends
trimmed
6 Slices Bacon, sliced
1/3 Cup Parmesan cheese,
grated
As Needed Bacon Grease

DIRECTIONS:

On your work surface, put down 2 large pieces of butcher's twine. Perpendicular to twine, put butterfly pork loin.
With the Traeger Pork and Poultry Rub, season the inside of the pork loin.
Layer all the ingredients on one end of the loin in a line, starting with the chopped walnuts, craisins, oregano, thyme, and asparagus.
Attach the bacon and add the parmesan cheese to the top.
Starting with all the fillings at the top, carefully roll up the pork loin and secure it with butcher's twine on both ends.
In the stored bacon grease, roll the pork loin and season the outside with more pork and poultry shake.
Set the temperature to 180 ° F when ready to cook and preheat for 15 minutes, lid closed. Put the stuffed loin of pork straight on the grill grill and smoke for 1 hour.
Remove the loin from the pork; raise the temperature to 350 ° F and allow it to preheat.
For around 30 to 45 minutes or until the temperature reads 135 ° F on an instant-read thermometer, put the loin back on the Traeger and grill.
Shift the pork loin to a plate with aluminum foil and tent it. Until slicing and serving, let it rest for 15 minutes. Enjoy! Enjoy!

Traeger Smoked Sausage

SERVING	PREP TIME	COOK TIME	PELLETS
4	30 MINS	3 HOURS	MESQUITE

Pork to fork wood-fired goodness. Ground pork, onion, garlic and ground mustard combine well for this homemade mesquite smoked sausage. You never go back to the store-bought-in-store.

INGREDIENTS:

3 Pound ground pork
1/2 Tablespoon ground mustard
1 Tablespoon onion powder
1 Tablespoon garlic powder
1 Teaspoon pink curing salt
1 Tablespoon salt
4 Teaspoon black pepper
1/2 Cup ice water
Hog casings, soaked and rinsed in cold water

DIRECTIONS:

Combine the meat and seasonings in a medium bowl, then blend well.

Add ice water to the meat and blend until it is blended with hands that work quickly.

Place the mixture in a sausage stuffer and follow the operating instructions given by the manufacturer. Use caution not to overstuff or it might burst the casing.

Determine your ideal length of attachment and pinch and twist a few times or tie it off until all the meat is stuffed. For each connection, repeat.

When ready to cook, set the temperature of the Traeger to 225 ° F and preheat for 15 minutes, lid closed. If available, use Super Smoke for the optimal flavor.

Place the connections directly on the grill grill and cook for 1 to 2 hours or until the temperature inside is 155 ° F. Before slicing, let the sausage rest for a few minutes. Enjoy! Enjoy!

3-2-1 BBQ Baby Back Ribs

INGREDIENTS:

2 Rack baby back pork ribs
1/3 Cup yellow mustard
1/2 Cup apple juice, divided
1 Tablespoon Worcestershire sauce
To Taste Traeger Pork & Poultry Rub
1/2 Cup dark brown sugar
1/3 Cup honey, warmed
1 Cup Traeger 'Que BBQ Sauce

SERVING	PREP TIME	COOK TIME	PELLETS
6	15 MINS	6 HOURS	HICKORY

Our famously simple 3-2-1 ribs recipe can turn the envy of the neighborhood into your rib game. Without losing any taste, this super easy recipe takes all the confusion out of making ribs. Start by smoking the ribs for 3 hours, then cook for 2 hours inside the foil and finish by removing it from the foil for up to an hour and brushing it with the sauce.

DIRECTIONS:

If your butcher has not already done so, by working the tip of a butter knife or a screwdriver under the membrane over the middle bone, extract the thin silverskin membrane from the bone-side of the ribs. To get a good grip, use paper towels, then cut the membrane off.

Combine the mustard, 1/4 cup apple juice (reserve the rest) and the Worcestershire sauce in a small bowl. On both sides of the ribs, spread the mixture thinly and season with Traeger Pork & Poultry Rub. When ready to cook, set the temperature of the Traeger to 180 º F and preheat for 15 minutes, lid closed. Smoke the ribs for 3 hours, meat-side up.

Switch them to a rimmed baking sheet after the ribs have smoked for 3 hours and raise the temperature of the grill to 225 º F.

Tear off four long, heavy-duty aluminum foil sheets. To hold the liquid sealed, top with a rack of ribs and pull up the sides. Sprinkle on the rack with half the brown sugar, then top with half the honey and half the apple juice left over. When you want more tender ribs, use a little more apple juice. On top, lay another piece of foil and crimp the edges tightly so that there is no leakage. With the remaining rack of ribs, repeat.

Put the foiled ribs back on the grill and cook for an extra 2 hours.

Remove the foil from the ribs carefully and brush the ribs with Traeger'Que Sauce on both sides. Cast the foil off. Arrange the ribs directly on the barbecue grill and continue to grill for an additional 30 to 60 minutes before the sauce tightens.

Before serving, let the ribs rest for a few minutes. Enjoy! Enjoy!

Cocktails Recipes

FOR WOOD PELLET SMOKER GRILLS

Smoked Margarita

SERVING	PREP TIME	COOK TIME	PELLETS
1	10 MINS	10 MINS	CHERRY

This margarita stands out from the rest because of its grilled, sugar-coated limes and Traeger Smoked Simple Syrup. For your next get-together, make a pitcher to share.

INGREDIENTS:

12 Whole lime wedges, slit in center
1/2 Cup turbinado sugar
1 1/2 Cup Fresh Squeezed Lime Juice from Grilled Limes
3 Cup silver tequila
1 1/2 Cup Cointreau
3/4 Cup Traeger Smoked Simple Syrup, plus more to taste
1/2 Cup Traeger Bloody Mary Cocktail Salt
lime wedge, for garnish

DIRECTIONS:

When ready to cook, set the temperature of the Traeger to 500 ° F and preheat for 15 minutes, lid closed.

Halve the limes, dip in turbinado sugar and put flesh side down on the preheated grill.

5 minutes of grilling or before you get a little char. Take the limes off the grill and juice them.

Using a pitcher to add lime juice, tequila, Cointreau and Traeger Smoked Simple Syrup. Stir to blend.

Place Traeger Bloody Mary Cocktail Salt just wide enough to match the glass rim in a low-sided dish.

Run the lime around each rim of the bottle, dip the rim in the salt and fill the glass with ice.

Pour in the margarita mixture and garnish with a slice of lime. Enjoy! Enjoy!

Traeger Paloma Cocktail

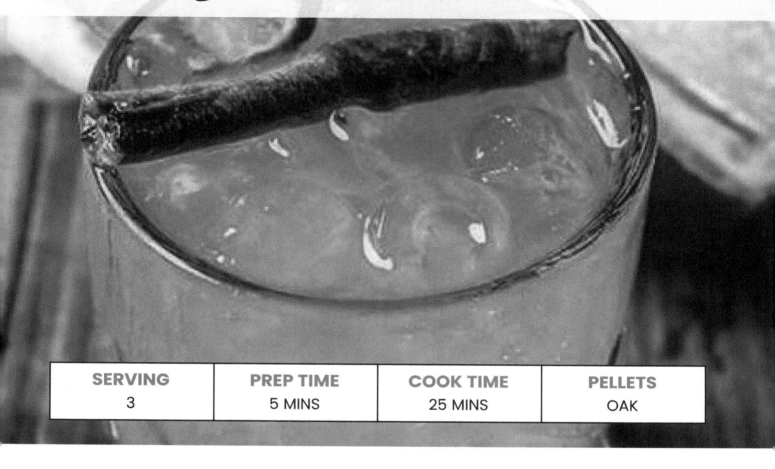

SERVING	PREP TIME	COOK TIME	PELLETS
3	5 MINS	25 MINS	OAK

For a cocktail mixer you won't want to mess with, put cinnamon sticks in grapefruit halves, glaze with Traeger Simple Syrup and barbecue to caramelized perfection.

INGREDIENTS:

2 grapefruit, halved
As Needed Traeger Smoked
Simple Syrup
5 Stick cinnamon
1 1/2 Ounce reposado tequila
1/2 Ounce lime juice
1/2 Ounce Traeger Smoked
Simple Syrup
grilled lime, for garnish
cinnamon stick, for garnish

DIRECTIONS:

Set the Traeger temperature to 350 ° F when ready to cook and preheat, the lid closed for 15 minutes.
Grapefruit Juice Grilled: Split 2 grapefruits in half. Place each grapefruit half with a cinnamon stick and glaze with Traeger Smoked Simple Syrup. Place it on the grill grill and cook for 20 minutes or until the edges begin to burn and grill marks are obtained. Remove and let cool from the sun. Squeeze and strain the juice after the grapefruits have cooled. The juice can yield 10 to 12 ounces.
Put the tequila, lime juice, Traeger Smoked Simple Syrup and 2 ounces of grilled grapefruit juice in a mixing glass.
Shake and add ice. Strain in an old-fashioned glass over ice.
To garnish, add a grilled lime slice and a cinnamon stick. Enjoy! Enjoy!

Garden Gimlet Cocktail

SERVING	PREP TIME	COOK TIME	PELLETS
1	5 MINS	45 MINS	PECAN

Enjoy a sweet summertime sip. Rosemary syrup, lime, cucumber and vodka from smoked lemon & honey make for a sweet and earthy refresher.

INGREDIENTS:

1 Cup honey
2 lemons, zested
2 Sprig rosemary, plus more for garnish
1/4 Cup water
2 Slices cucumber
3/4 Ounce lime juice
1 1/2 Ounce vodka

DIRECTIONS:

Set the Traeger temperature to 180 ° F when ready to cook and preheat, the lid closed for 15 minutes. If available, use Super Smoke for the optimal flavor.
Dilute 1 cup of honey by adding 1/4 cup of water to a shallow pan to make smoked lemon and rosemary honey syrup. Add the lemon zest and 2 rosemary sprigs.
Place the pan on the grill and smoke for 45 minutes to an hour. Remove from fire, cool and strain.

Combine the cucumber, lime juice and 1 ounce of smoked lemon and rosemary honey syrup in a mixing glass.
In a coupé glass, apply ice, shake and double strain after muddling.
Garnish with a rosemary sprig. Enjoy! Enjoy!

Smoked Plum and Thyme Fizz Cocktail

SERVING	PREP TIME	COOK TIME	PELLETS
1	15 MINS	1 HOUR	MAPLE

You tried this bubbly drink. It's thyme. A homemade smoked plum and thyme simple syrup is hit with vodka and club soda for the taste you can throw back time and time again.

INGREDIENTS:

3 Plums, fresh
1 thyme sprigs
1 Cup Traeger Smoked Simple Syrup
Fluid Ounce vodka
3/4 Fluid Ounce lemon juice

DIRECTIONS:

When ready to cook, set the temperature of the grill to 180 ° F and preheat for 15 minutes, lid closed.

Cut 3 plums in half and remove the pit. Place the plum halves directly on the grill grate and smoke for 25 minutes. For the Plum and Thyme Simple Syrup: After 25 minutes , remove plums from the grill and cut into quarters. Add plums and thyme sprigs to 1 cup of Traeger Smoked Simple Syrup. For 45 minutes, smoke the mixture. Remove and strain from the grill, and let cool.

Add 2 oz of vodka, 0.75 oz of fresh lemon juice and 1 oz of smoked plum and thyme syrup to the mixing glass for the cocktail. Shake and add ice.

Top off with club soda and garnish with a piece of thyme and a slice of smoked plum. Pour over clean ice. Enjoy! Enjoy!

Smoked and Bubz Cocktail

SERVING	PREP TIME	COOK TIME	PELLETS
1	5 MINS	45 MINS	PECAN

Before mixing it with sparkling wine and topping it off with a lemon twist for your new favorite cocktail, smoke low and slow pomegranate juice on the Traeger.

INGREDIENTS:

8 Ounce POM Juice
1 Cup pomegranate seeds
3 Ounce sparkling white wine
1 lemon twist, for garnish
1 Teaspoon pomegranate seeds

DIRECTIONS:

Set the Traeger temperature to 180 ° F when ready to cook and preheat, the lid closed for 15 minutes. If available, use Super Smoke for the optimal flavor.

For Smoked Pomegranate Juice: Pour into a shallow sheet pan with POM juice and a cup of pomegranate seeds. Smoke for 45 minutes on the Traeger. Remove the grill, strain, discard the seeds and let sit until the seeds are cooled.

In a champagne flute, add 1-1/2 ounces of the smoked pomegranate juice to the rim.

To garnish, add sparkling white wine, a couple of fresh pomegranate seeds and a lemon twist. Enjoy! Enjoy!

Traeger Gin & Tonic

SERVING	PREP TIME	COOK TIME	PELLETS
3	10 MINS	45 MINS	PECAN

Traeger's Gin & Tonic takes an old-school favorite and incorporates grilled oranges and smoked berries into the smoke era.

INGREDIENTS:

1/4 Cup berries
1 orange, sliced
2 Tablespoon granulated sugar
1 1/2 Ounce gin
1/2 Cup tonic water
1 Sprig fresh mint, for garnish

DIRECTIONS:

When ready to cook, set the temperature of the Traeger to 180 ° F and preheat for 15 minutes, lid closed. If available, use Super Smoke for the optimal flavor.

For the Smoked Berries: On a sheet pan, spread the mixed fresh berries and put them directly on the grill. Remove from the grill for 30 minutes, then smoke.

For Orange Slices: Raise the temperature of the grill to 450 ° F and preheat for 15 minutes with the lid closed.

Mix the orange slices with the granulated sugar and put them directly on the grill. Cook for approximately 5 minutes, rotating once or until grill marks have formed in the slices.

In a glass, pour the gin, add the ice and berries, then cover it with tonic water. Garnish with a sprig of fresh mint and a wheel of grilled orange. Enjoy! Enjoy!

Smoked Barnburner Cocktail

SERVING	PREP TIME	COOK TIME	PELLETS
1	5 MINS	45 MINS	APPLE

Sip on that sweet and smoky cocktail. This cocktail based on tequila combines smoked raspberries, sweet simple syrup and a little acidity for a perfectly balanced drink that you will reach for over and over again.

INGREDIENTS:

1 Tub fresh raspberries
3/4 Ounce smoked raspberry syrup
1 1/2 Ounce reposado tequila
1/2 Fluid Ounce lime juice
1/2 Fluid Ounce lemon juice
1 Pieces grilled lime wheel, for garnish

DIRECTIONS:

When you're ready to cook, fire the Smoke Traeger grill.
Place the fresh raspberries on a grill mat, and smoke for 30 minutes on the Traeger. Place them in a shallow sheet pan with 1: 1 simple syrup after the raspberries have been smoked.
On the grill rack, put the sheet pan and smoke for 45 minutes. Remove and let cool from the grill. When ready to use, refrigerate.
In a mixing glass, combine all the ingredients with ice. Shake and pour over ice that's clean. Garnish with smoked raspberries and a candied lime wheel on the grill. Enjoy Enjoy!

Smoked Kenyucky Mule

SERVING	PREP TIME	COOK TIME	PELLETS
1	5 MINS	1 MIN	APPLE

Light, refreshing and summer-perfect. This drink offers a lime juice kick to High West whiskey and sweetens the deal with Traeger Smoked Simple Syrup and ginger beer.

INGREDIENTS:

2 Fluid Ounce High West Whiskey
1/2 Fluid Ounce lime juice
1/2 Fluid Ounce Traeger Smoked Simple Syrup
4 Fluid Ounce ginger beer
As Needed fresh mint leaves
1 lime wedge, for garnish

DIRECTIONS:

Pour in bourbon, lime juice, and Traeger Smoked Simple Syrup and fill an 8 oz glass with ice. Stir to blend.
Round off with a beer with ginger. Give it another stir and garnish with a lime wedge and mint. Enjoy! Enjoy!

Smoked Hot Toddy

SERVING	PREP TIME	COOK TIME	PELLETS
1	10 MINS	30 MINS	HICKORY

Warm up your winter nights with this classic whiskey cocktail with a smokin'take on.

INGREDIENTS:

8 Fluid Ounce lemonade
1 mint tea bag
1 peach tea bag
1 green tea bag
4 Fluid Ounce whiskey
1 lemon wedges
1 cinnamon stick

DIRECTIONS:

Set temperature to high when ready to cook and preheat, lid closed for 15 minutes.

Into a shallow baking dish, pour lemonade and put directly on the grill grill. Cook for about 20-30 minutes, until the temperature reaches 200 ° F.

Take the lemonade off the grill and pour it into a bottle. Steep tea bags, 2-4 minutes of hot lemonade. Remove the bags of tea and pour the whisky in.

If needed, garnish with sliced lemon and a cinnamon stick. Enjoy! Enjoy!

Smoked Pineapple Hotel Nacional Cocktail

SERVING	PREP TIME	COOK TIME	PELLETS
1	4 HOURS	30 MINS	OAK

Have a seat, relax, and stay for a while. This smoked twist is damn good for the popular Cuban cocktail. You're not going to know what hit you ... before you get hit.

INGREDIENTS:

1 Whole Pineapple, sliced
1/4 Cup water
1/4 Cup sugar
1 1/2 Fluid Ounce white rum
3/4 Fluid Ounce lime juice
3/4 Fluid Ounce Pineapple Syrup
1/2 Fluid Ounce Apricot Brandy
1 Dash Angostura bitters

DIRECTIONS:

For syrup: when ready to cook, set the temperature of the grill to 180 ° F and preheat for 15 minutes with the lid closed.

Trim the pineapple on both sides, discard the ends. Break the pineapple into around 3/4 "thick slices. It doesn't hurt to leave it on. Don't think about the skin. Put the pineapple slices on the grill and smoke on each side for about 15 minutes.

Combine water and sugar in a saucepan over low heat while the pineapple is smoking, stirring continuously, until the sugar has dissolved. Put the syrup in a large tub, then set it aside.

Cut each slice into eight or so wedges when the pineapple has finished cooking and add the wedges with the simple syrup to the cup, toss to coat and cover.

Leave the mixture to macerate in the refrigerator for at least 4 hours (or up to 24), stirring from time to time.

Strain the syrup into a clean bowl through a fine-mesh strainer and press on the pineapple with a ladle to extract as much liquid as possible. You can bottle and refrigerate the syrup for up to 4 days.

To make the drink: In a cocktail shaker or mixing glass, add rum, lime juice, pineapple syrup, apricot brandy, and bitters. Fill the ice cubes and shake until they're cold.

Strain into a bottle of a frozen cocktail. Garnish with a wheel of lime and serve. Enjoy Enjoy!

Smoked Sangria Recipe

SERVING	PREP TIME	COOK TIME	PELLETS
1	20 MINS	45 MINS	PECAN

With Traeger's recipe for Smoked Sangria, pour up some smoky and fruity taste. Start by smoking Grand Marnier, cranberries and simple syrup right on the pit grill. To put it all together, add apples, limes and cinnamon sticks with red wine..

INGREDIENTS:

1/4 Cup Grand Marnier
1/4 Cup Traeger Smoked Simple Syrup
1 Cup Cranberries, fresh
1 Whole apple, sliced
2 Whole limes, sliced
4 cinnamon stick
1 Bottle red wine
As Needed soda water

DIRECTIONS:

Set the temperature to 180 ° F when ready to cook and preheat for 15 minutes with the lid closed.

Combine the Grand Marnier, Traeger Simple Syrup and cranberries in a shallow dish and put them directly on the grill.

Smoke for 30-45 minutes or until the desired smoke from the liquid picks up. Remove from the grill and place to cool in the refrigerator.

When the mixture has cooled, put the red wine in a large pitcher. To the pitcher, add sliced apples, limes, cinnamon sticks and ice.

If needed, top with soda water. Enjoy! Enjoy!

Smoky Mountain Bramble Cocktail

SERVING	PREP TIME	COOK TIME	PELLETS
3	20 MINS	20 MINS	HICKORY

Healthy vibes and good times with this concoction are just a shot away. To make a refreshing summer cocktail, we mixed vodka with smoked blackberries, alpine liqueur, lemon juice and plain syrup.

INGREDIENTS:

8 Ounce blackberries
1 Cup water
1 Cup sugar
5 blackberries
1 1/2 Fluid Ounce vodka
3/4 Fluid Ounce Alpine Preserve
3/4 Fluid Ounce lemon juice
1/2 Fluid Ounce Smoked Blackberry Syrup

DIRECTIONS:

Set the temperature to 180 ° F when ready to cook and preheat for 15 minutes with the lid closed. If available, use Super Smoke for the optimal flavor.

Put the blackberries on a grill mat and smoke for 15-20 minutes to make Smoked Blackberry Simple Syrup. In a small saucepan, mix the water and sugar and warm over medium heat until well mixed.

Remove from the heat and put in the plain syrup and macerate 2/3 of the blackberries. Strain via a strainer of fine mesh and store for up to 14 days.

Muddle 4-5 blackberries in a cocktail shaker to make your cocktail: Add the vodka, alpine preserve, ginger, and blackberry syrup, which is smoked. Attach ice and vigorously shake. Into an old style glass double pressure.

Garnish with smoked blackberries with a twist of lemon. Enjoy Enjoy!

Vegetarian Recipes

FOR WOOD PELLET SMOKER GRILLS

Smoked Pasta Salad

SERVING	PREP TIME	COOK TIME	PELLETS
8	30 MINS	20 MINS	APPLE

To this picnic classic, we're adding some wood-fired flavor. Before being tossed with pasta in a light Italian vinaigrette, tomatoes, fresh mozzarella, peppers, and salami get a kiss of Traeger smoke.

INGREDIENTS:

8 Ounce mozzarella cheese
1 Pound Salami
1 Jar Roasted Red Peppers, sliced
3 Cup Cherry tomatoes, sliced
3/4 Cup black olives
1/4 Cup chopped flat-leaf parsley
1 red onion, diced
To Taste Jarred Pepperoncini Peppers, thinly sliced
1 Pound Rotini Pasta
1/2 Cup red wine vinegar
1/2 Cup extra-virgin olive oil
3 Clove garlic, minced
1 Tablespoon honey
1 Tablespoon Italian Seasoning
To Taste black pepper
To Taste kosher salt

DIRECTIONS:

Set the temperature to 180 ° F when ready to cook and preheat for 15 minutes with the lid closed. If available, use Super Smoke for the optimal flavor.

On a sheet tray, put all ingredients except the pasta. Place the tray and smoke on the grill for 10 minutes. Remove and set aside from the barbecue.

Over high heat, put a large pot of water and bring it to a boil. To the water, add a big spoonful of salt. Stir in the dried pasta and cook according to the al dente package instructions. When the pasta is boiling, in a small cup, whisk all the vinaigrette ingredients and set aside.

Drain the pasta and rinse in a colander of cold water. Place the pasta in a large mixing bowl and shake off the excess water.

Chop all the ingredients from the salad. Place all the ingredients in a pasta mixing bowl. To coat, pour the vinaigrette over the top and toss well. As required, season with salt and pepper.

Until eating, put it in the refrigerator to cool for 30 minutes. Enjoy! Enjoy!

Roasted Cauliflower

SERVING	PREP TIME	COOK TIME	PELLETS
2	15 MINS	30 MINS	MAPLE

Cauliflower is typically not on the "most wanted side dish" list by itself, but roasted with the right spices and flavored with flavorful smoke will have everyone asking for more. In order to top it off, did we mention melted Parmesan? You will now have to make enough for everyone to call for seconds.

INGREDIENTS:

1 Head Cauliflower, fresh
2 Tablespoon extra-virgin olive oil
2 Clove garlic clove
1 1/4 Teaspoon smoked paprika
1/2 Teaspoon salt
1/2 Teaspoon black pepper
1 Cup Parmesan cheese

DIRECTIONS:

Set the temperature to 180 ° F when ready to cook and preheat with the lid closed for 15 minutes. If available, use Super Smoke for the optimal flavor.

Cut the cauliflower into medium florets and put it on a tray of sheets. For 20 minutes, move the sheet tray to the grill and smoke.

Mix all the ingredients together, except for the Parmesan cheese, while the cauliflower is smoked.

Cut the cauliflower after 20 minutes. Increase the temperature of the grill to 450 ° F and preheat it for 15 minutes with the lid closed.

Toss the cauliflower with the spice mixture while the grill reaches temperature, and put it back on the sheet tray.

Put the Traeger back on and roast for 10 minutes or until the color is good and golden brown.

Sprinkle the Parmesan over each piece in the last few minutes of cooking, closing the lid until the cheese is melted. Enjoy! Enjoy!

Smoked Hummus with Roasted Vegetables

SERVING	PREP TIME	COOK TIME	PELLETS
4	15 MINS	40 MINS	HICKORY

Apply some smokin 'spice to this balanced snack. Seasoned with aromatic spices such as tahini, garlic, and smoked paprika, this homemade hummus is smoked and served aside for the perfect dip with roasted veggies.

INGREDIENTS:

1 1/2 Cup Chickpeas
333/1000 Cup tahini
1 Tablespoon garlic, minced
2 Tablespoon extra-virgin olive oil
1 Teaspoon salt
4 Tablespoon lemon juice
1 red onion, sliced
2 Cup butternut squash
2 Cup Cauliflower, cut into florets
2 Cup fresh Brussels sprouts
2 Whole Portobello Mushroom
4 Tablespoon extra-virgin olive oil
To Taste salt
To Taste black pepper

DIRECTIONS:

When ready to cook, set the temperature of the grill to 180 ° F and preheat for 15 minutes, lid closed.
Drain and rinse the chickpeas for the hummus and spread them out on a sheet tray. For 15-20 minutes or to the optimal amount of smoke, put the tray in the grill grate and smoke.
Combine the smoked chickpeas, tahini, garlic, olive oil , salt, and lemon juice in the bowl of a food processor and process until well combined but not completely smooth. Transfer to and reserve a cup.
Increase the grill temperature to high and pre-heat.
For vegetables: Sprinkle veggies with olive oil and spread on a tray of sheets. Put in the grill sheet tray and roast veggies for 15-20 minutes until lightly browned and cooked through.
Place hummus in a serving bowl or dish for serving and top with roasted veggies.
Add olive oil and serve with pita bread. Enjoy! Enjoy!

Homemade Smoked Ketchup

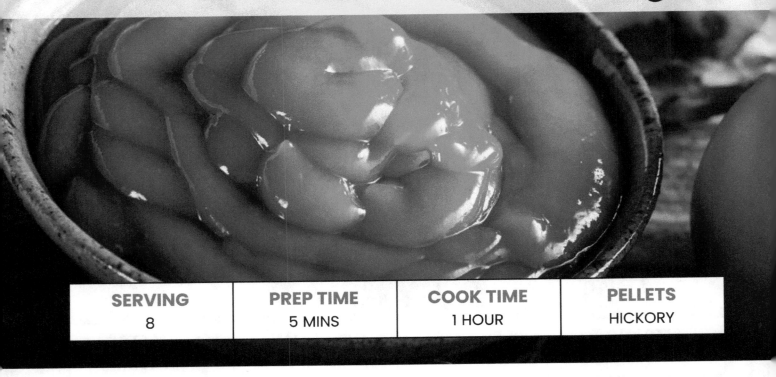

SERVING	PREP TIME	COOK TIME	PELLETS
8	5 MINS	1 HOUR	HICKORY

Forget the stuff purchased from the supermarket, and lay our version on thick. A ketchup of epic proportions is made with smoked tomatoes and a combination of spices.

INGREDIENTS:

2 Tablespoon olive oil, divided
2 Can (28 oz) can whole peeled tomatoes
3 Clove garlic
1 yellow onion, peeled and quartered
2 Tablespoon tomato paste
1/4 Cup apple cider vinegar
2 Tablespoon Worcestershire sauce
1/8 Teaspoon ground cloves
1/4 Teaspoon cayenne pepper
4 Tablespoon brown sugar
To Taste salt

DIRECTIONS:

When ready to cook, set the temperature of the Traeger to 225 F and preheat for 15 minutes with the lid closed. If available, use Super Smoke for the optimal flavor.

Toss the tomatoes with 1 tablespoon of olive oil and spread on a baking sheet.

Place the tray straight on the grill and smoke for 1 hour. Remove and set aside from the barbecue.

Over medium heat, heat the remaining olive oil in a medium sauce pan. Connect the garlic and onion and cook for 1 minute.

Attach the tomato paste and cook for an additional minute before the tomato paste turns rusty.

With the addition of smoked tomatoes, apple cider vinegar and Worcestershire sauce, deglaze.

To pick up all the bits at the bottom of the pan, stir with a wooden spoon. Bring to a boil and incorporate ground cloves and cayenne.

Cook for 20 minutes, until the back of the spoon is thick enough to cover it.

To mix, add brown sugar and stir.

Move the mixture and puree to a blender until smooth. Adjust seasoning to taste with salt.

Transfer to the drying and cooling container in the refrigerator..

Use burgers, hot dogs and fries to serve. Enjoy! Enjoy!

Smoked Scalloped Potatoes

SERVING	PREP TIME	COOK TIME	PELLETS
6	10 MINS	1 HOUR	CHERRY

These potatoes are oozing with a savory taste, cheesy, creamy and cherry wood smoked. Scalloped potatoes are highly layered with a classic cast-iron cheddar cream sauce and baked to bubbly perfection.

INGREDIENTS:

2 Tablespoon butter, softened
1 Cup heavy cream
1/2 Cup milk
2 Tablespoon flour
2 Clove garlic, chopped
4 russet potatoes, peeled and thinly sliced
As Needed kosher salt
As Needed coarse ground black pepper
1/2 Cup grated medium cheddar cheese
1/2 Cup grated sharp white cheddar

DIRECTIONS:

Set the temperature of the Traeger to 375 degrees F when ready to cook and preheat, lid closed, for 15 minutes.
Spread on the bottom and sides of a 9-inch cast iron skillet with butter.
In a cup, mix the cream, milk, flour, and garlic together.
Sprinkle with salt and pepper, layer 1/4th of the potatoes in the pan, and pour 1/4th of the sauce mixture over the potatoes. Repeat 3 more times over.
Grill the potatoes and cook for 50 minutes.
With both cheeses, top the potatoes evenly and cook for an extra 10 minutes or until the potatoes are fork tender.
Remove and serve from the grill. Enjoy! Enjoy!

Smoked Pico De Gallo

SERVING	PREP TIME	COOK TIME	PELLETS
4	10 MINS	30 MINS	SIGNATURE

Who knew it would be so good with smoked tomatoes? Chef Timothy did, however. Pair it with almost everything. Damn it, bring it on cardboard and you're going to have a winner. It's so sweet.

INGREDIENTS:

3 Cup diced Roma tomatoes
1 jalapeño, diced
1/2 red onion, diced
1/2 Bunch cilantro, finely chopped
2 lime, juiced
To Taste salt
To Taste olive oil

DIRECTIONS:

Set the Traeger temperature to 180 ° F when ready to cook and preheat, the lid closed for 15 minutes. If available, use Super Smoke for the optimal flavor.

Place the diced tomatoes, spreading them into a thin layer on a small sheet pan. Directly put the sheet pan on the grill and smoke for 30 minutes.

Toss all the ingredients in a medium bowl when the tomatoes are done and finish with lime juice, salt and olive oil to taste. Serving and loving!

Pro Team member Chef Timothy Hollingsworth given this recipe.

Smoked Olives

SERVING	PREP TIME	COOK TIME	PELLETS
6	10 MINS	20 MINS	CHERRY

Pop the goodness into your mouth. The perfect pairing of these olives with smoke is.

INGREDIENTS:

1 Pound mixed olives
1 Quart extra-virgin olive oil
1 Whole orange zest
1 Whole lemon zest
1/2 Tablespoon red pepper flakes
1/2 Tablespoon dried fennel seed
3 Whole dried bay leaves
4 Whole thyme sprigs
4 Whole rosemary sprigs

DIRECTIONS:

On Smoke, start the Traeger grill when ready to cook and leave the temperature to the setting of the smoke.
Place the olives in a roasting pan and put them on the grill. Smoke for 20 to 30 minutes or until there is a smoky taste in the olives.
Remove from the grill and cool when the olives attain the desired smokiness. Smoked olives, olive oil, orange and lemon zest, red pepper flakes, fennel, bay leaves, thyme and rosemary are mixed until cooled. Store in an airtight jar to ensure the submersion of all olives.
Serve as part of the Traeger Ultimate Picnic Spread or with your favourite dishes. Enjoy Enjoy!

Grilled Zucchini Squash Spears

SERVING	PREP TIME	COOK TIME	PELLETS
6	5 MINS	10 MINS	OAK

Bring the crew together and serve them this recipe for grilled zucchini squash spears and a host of spices for a smokin' glass of goodness.

INGREDIENTS:

4 medium zucchini
2 tbsp olive oil
1 tbsp cherry vinegar
2 springs thyme, leaves pulled
salt and pepper, to taste

DIRECTIONS:

The zucchini should be washed and each end cut off. Break each of them into halves, then cut each of them into thirds. In a medium Ziploc container, mix the remaining ingredients and add the lances. To coat the zucchini, flip and combine well.

Set the temperature to 350 F when ready to cook and preheat for 15 minutes with the lid closed.

Remove the spears from the bag and put the cut side down directly on the grill grate.

Cook on each side for 3-4 minutes, until grill marks appear and the zucchini is tender.

Remove from the grill and finish, if needed, with more thyme leaves. Enjoy! Enjoy!

Grilled Veggie Sandwich

SERVING	PREP TIME	COOK TIME	PELLETS
4	30 MINS	30 MINS	PECAN

Say goodbye to the blue box and hello to the grilled veggie sandwich.

INGREDIENTS:

smoked hummus
1-1/2 cups chickpeas
1/3 cup tahini
1 tbsp minced garlic
2 tbsp olive oil
1 tsp kosher salt
4 tbsp lemon juice
grilled veggie sandwich
1 small eggplant, sliced into strips
1 small zucchini, sliced into strips
1 small yellow squash, sliced into strips
2 large portobello mushrooms
olive oil
salt and pepper to taste
2 heirloom tomatoes, sliced
1 bunch basil, leaves pulled
4 ciabatta buns
1/2 cup ricotta
juice of 1 lemon
1 garlic clove minced
salt and pepper to taste

DIRECTIONS:

Set the temperature to 180 F when ready to cook and preheat for 15 minutes with the lid closed.

Drain and rinse the chickpeas for the hummus and spread them out on a sheet tray. For 15-20 minutes or to the optimal amount of smoke, put the tray in the grill grate and smoke.

Combine the smoked chickpeas, tahini, garlic, olive oil , salt and lemon juice in the bowl of a food processor and process until well blended but not completely smooth. Transfer to and reserve a cup.

Increase the temp of the grill to high (400-500 ?? F).

Toss the olive oil, lemon juice , salt and pepper with the eggplant, zucchini, squash, and portobellos. On the grill grill grill mushrooms gill side up, put the veggies directly. Cook veggies (10-15 minutes for sliced veggies, 20-25 minutes for mushrooms) until grill marks grow and veggies are tender.

Combine the ricotta, lemon juice, garlic, salt and pepper in a small bowl as the vegetables cook.

Break the buns of ciabatta in half and open up. On one hand, spread hummus and on the other, ricotta. Stack the grilled vegetables and top with the basil and tomatoes. Enjoy! Enjoy!

Grilled Fingerling Potato Salad

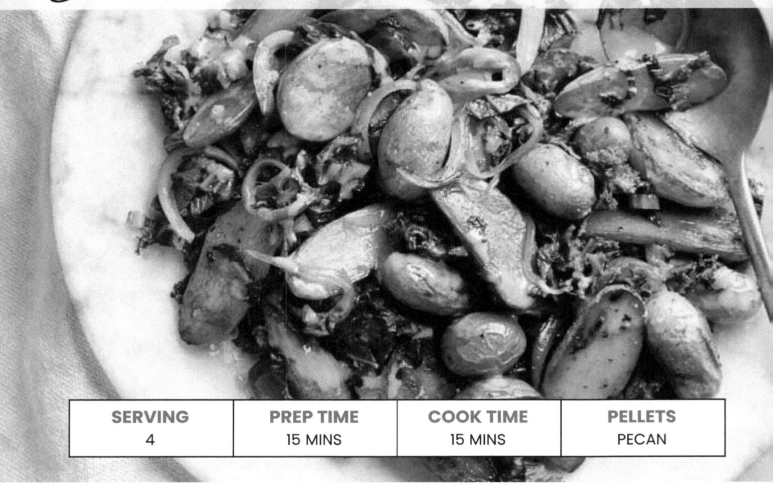

SERVING	PREP TIME	COOK TIME	PELLETS
4	15 MINS	15 MINS	PECAN

Apply some grilled fingerling potato salad diet. For full-bodied flavor, smokin' recipe infuses pecanwood richness into your food that you can keep coming back to.

INGREDIENTS:

1-1/2 lbs. fingerling potatoes cut in half lengthwise
10 scallions
2/3 cup evoo (extra virgin olive oil), divided use
2 tbsp rice vinegar
2 tsp lemon juice
1 small jalapeno, sliced
2 tsp kosher salt

DIRECTIONS:

Set temperature to high when ready to cook and preheat, lid closed for 15 minutes.

Brush the oil with the scallions and place them on the grill. Cook for approximately 2-3 minutes, until lightly charred. Remove and cool down. Slice and set aside until the scallions have cooled.

Brush the fingerlings with oil, then salt and pepper (reserving 1/3 of a cup for later use). Place cut side down on the grill for around 4-5 minutes until cooked through.

Mix the remaining 1/3 cup of olive oil, rice vinegar , salt, and lemon juice in a bowl, then add the scallions, potatoes, and jalapeo slices.

Season with pepper and salt, and serve. Enjoy! Enjoy!

Seafood Recipes

FOR WOOD PELLET SMOKER GRILLS

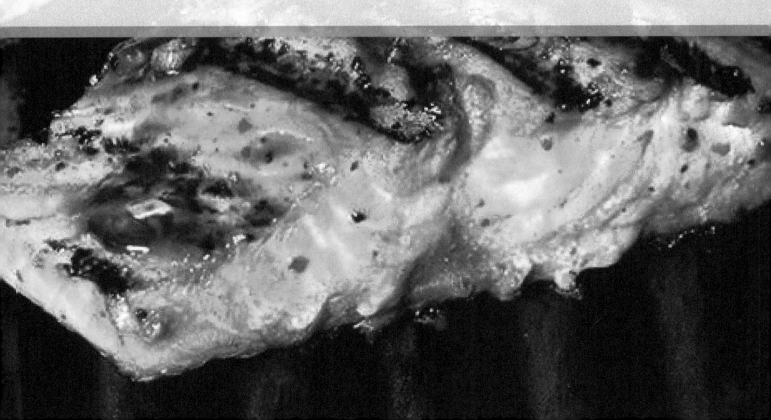

Smoked Fish Chowder

SERVING	PREP TIME	COOK TIME	PELLETS
4	15 MINS	1 HOUR	ALDER

The beloved Boston clam chowder from Fenway Park is smoked in this recipe. Vanquish those fishy chowder ideas, this recipe uses Traeger smoked salmon robustly so that it is tasty and mild.

INGREDIENTS:

12 Ounce (1-1/2 to 2 lb) skin-on salmon fillet, preferably wild-caught
As Needed Traeger Fin & Feather Rub
2 Corn Husks
3 Slices Bacon, sliced
4 Can Cream of Potato Soup, Condensed
3 Cup whole milk
8 Ounce cream cheese
3 green onions, thinly sliced
2 Teaspoon hot sauce

DIRECTIONS:

When ready to cook, set the temperature of the grill to 180 ° F and preheat for 15 minutes, lid closed.

On salmon, sprinkle Traeger Fin & Feather rub as desired. On the grill grate, place the salmon skin-side down. 30 minutes to smoke.

Increase the temperature of the grill to 350 ° F.

For 30 minutes, cook the salmon, or until the fish flakes easily with a fork. (The exact time would depend on the fillet 's thickness.) The fish need not be turned around. To cool, move the salmon to a wire rack using a wide, thin spatula. Get the skin removed. (A day ahead, wrapped in plastic wrap and refrigerated, the salmon can be made.) Split and set aside into flakes.

Arrange the strips of corn and bacon on the grill shelf. Roast the corn and the bacon until the corn is cooked through and browned in spots, turning as required, and the bacon is crisp, about 15 minutes. (The salmon will be roasting as you do this.)

Meanwhile, in a large saucepan or Dutch oven on the stovetop, bring the cream of the potato soup and the milk to a boil over medium heat. Stir in the cream cheese gradually and whisk to mix. Chop the bacon into pieces and use the long strokes of a chef's knife to slice the maize off the cobs.

Apply the green onions to the broth. Stir the salmon in. Gently heat for 5 to 10 minutes. To taste, apply the hot sauce. Add more milk if the chowder is too thick. At once, serve. Enjoy Enjoy!

Smoked Trout

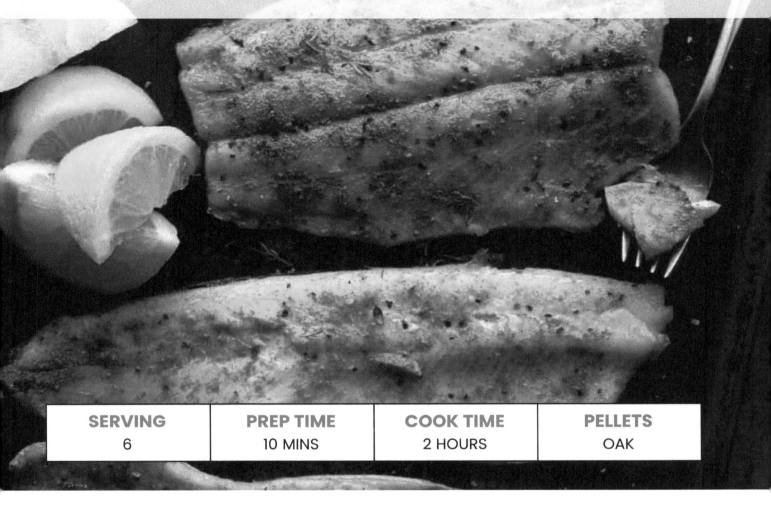

SERVING	PREP TIME	COOK TIME	PELLETS
6	10 MINS	2 HOURS	OAK

This simple smoked trout recipe helps the flavors of the fish and smoke to shine on their own. Only butterfly the trout, brine it for an hour, then let it smoke and eat it hot or cold.

INGREDIENTS:

Units of Measurement:
8 rainbow trout fillets
1 Gallon water
1/4 Cup salt
1/2 Cup brown sugar
1 Tablespoon black pepper
2 Tablespoon soy sauce

DIRECTIONS:

Clean the new fish with a butterfly.
Combine one gallon of water, brown sugar, soy sauce, salt and pepper and mix until the salt and sugar are fully dissolved. In the refrigerator, brine the trout for 60 minutes. When ready to cook, set the temperature of the Traeger to 225 ° F and preheat for 15 minutes, lid closed. If available, use Super Smoke for the optimal flavor.
Remove the brine from the fish and pat it dry. Place the fish directly on the grill, depending on the thickness of the trout, for 1-1/2 to 2 hours. When it becomes opaque and starts to flake, the fish is finished. Serve cold or hot. Enjoy! Enjoy!
When it becomes opaque and starts to flake, the finished. Serve cold or hot. Enjoy! Enjoy!

Smoked Salmon Sandwich

SERVING	PREP TIME	COOK TIME	PELLETS
4	1 DAY	3 HOUR	APPLE

This fish is as new as the water in which he swam. Enjoy this apple smoked salmon sandwich on a rustic ciabatta roll with creamy herb mayo, heirloom tomatoes, greens and topped with the tang of pickled onions.

INGREDIENTS:

4 Pound salmon
1 1/2 Cup salt
1 Cup brown sugar
1 Tablespoon juniper berries
4 bay leaves, crushed
1 Teaspoon black pepper
3/4 Cup red wine vinegar
1/2 Cup sugar
2 Tablespoon salt
2 red onion, sliced
1/2 Cup mayonnaise
1 Teaspoon Dill, fresh or dried
1 Teaspoon Tarragon, dried leaves
1 Teaspoon fresh parsley
1 Teaspoon Chives, fresh
4 Rolls, ciabatta
1 Cup Greens, fresh
2 Medium heirloom tomato

DIRECTIONS:

Smoked Salmon: Clean the salmon to ensure that all pin bones and scales are removed. Combine the salt, brown sugar, bay leaves, juniper berries (crushed), and black pepper.

Place it on the counter with a long piece of plastic wrap. On top of the plastic, spread 2/3 of the cure mixture then put salmon skin side down. Spread the remaining cure on top of the fillet, then carefully wrap the ends of the plastic wrap and fold them to ensure that the cure of the salmon is tightly protected.

Place the salmon on a baking sheet and cover it with another baking sheet. On top of the sheet pan, put something heavy so that the weight is spread evenly along the salmon fillets. Enable 24 hours to recover.

Take off the salmon side of the plastic wrap after 24 hours and clean the remaining cure. Pat the salmon dry, then on top of a sheet pan, lie flat on a cooling rack. Place in the refrigerator and allow to sit to shape the pellicle overnight. This will cause the smoke to cling to the salmon.

Set the temperature to 180 ° F when ready to cook and preheat for 15 minutes with the lid closed.

Set the skin-side-down salmon fillets on the grill. Smoke for 1-3 hours or until 150 ° F is reported by a thermometer inserted into the thickest part of the salmon. To ensure that it does not get above 160 ° F, make sure to closely track the temperature. Remove and set aside the salmon.

Combine the vinegar, sugar , and salt in a medium saucepan over medium-high heat while the salmon is cooking. Cook until the salt and sugar are dissolved and pour the sliced onions over them. Cover and refrigerate for a minimum of 1 hour before use.

Mix the mayo, the herbs and the salt and pepper in a small cup.

Smear herb mayo on both sides of the ciabatta roll to create the sandwich. Layers of smoked salmon, spring greens, pickled red onions, and tomatoes. Enjoy! Enjoy!

Smoked Seafood Ceviche

SERVING	PREP TIME	COOK TIME	PELLETS
4	20 MINS	1 HOUR	MESQUITE

Give seafood a smoke before marinating it in the bright and zesty citrus juices to add a deep and rich flavor. Season with lime and savory spices, and serve as an appetizer or main attraction.

INGREDIENTS:

1 Pound sea scallops, shucked
1 Pound shrimp, peeled and deveined
1 Tablespoon canola oil
1 lime, zested and juiced
1 lemon juice
1 orange, juiced
1 Teaspoon garlic powder
1 Teaspoon onion powder
2 Teaspoon salt
1/2 Teaspoon black pepper
1 diced avocado
1/2 red onion, diced
1 Tablespoon cilantro, finely chopped
1 Pinch red pepper flakes

DIRECTIONS:

Combine the shrimp, scallops and canola oil in a dish.
Set the grill temperature to 180 degrees F when ready to cook, and preheat for 15 minutes with the lid closed.
Arrange the grill with the shrimp and scallops and smoke them for 45 minutes. Prepare all the other ingredients when they are smoking, then put them in a big mixing bowl.
Turn the grill up to 325 and cook an further 5 minutes when the shrimp and scallops have stopped smoking, to ensure that they are completely cooked.
Cool the scallops and shrimp, then split them in half width-wise and mix with the bowl 's ingredients.
For at least 2-3 hours, refrigerate Ceviche to let the flavors blend. Serve with chips of corn.

Smoked Jacobsen Salt

SERVING	PREP TIME	COOK TIME	PELLETS
3	5 MINS	1 HOUR	HICKORY

Give this smoked Jacobsen salt a shake with meat and veggies. It's not an ordinary flavoring when the Traeger is smoked.

INGREDIENTS:

2 Pound Jacobsen Salt Co. Pure Kosher Sea Salt

DIRECTIONS:

Start the Traeger grill on Smoke when it's ready to cook before a fire is set up (4-5 minutes).

Place on a cooking sheet the 2 pounds of salt; spread evenly so all the salt is level.

Place the pan in the Traeger's back corner and smoke for a minimum of 1 hour.

After 1 hour, check the salt, and continue to smoke to your taste, if desired.

Hold it in a mason jar with a lid. Enjoy all you can with Traeger.

Smoked Salmon Flatbread

SERVING	PREP TIME	COOK TIME	PELLETS
4	15 MINS	6 MINS	ALDER

With our wood-fired flatbread topped with crème fraiche and smoked salmon, offer your usual bagel and lox the Traeger twist.

INGREDIENTS:

1 pizza dough
1/4 Cup Creme Fraiche
1/4 Cup Ricotta Cheese
To Taste salt
To Taste black pepper
As Needed chives, chopped
As Needed Smoked Salmon
As Needed capers, drained
As Needed extra-virgin olive oil

DIRECTIONS:

Set the grill temperature to high and preheat when ready to cook, the lid closed for 15 minutes.
Roll out your pizza dough, meanwhile.
Place the dough directly on the barbecue grill. You just need to cook it on one side for about 3 minutes.
Over the crust, scatter the creme fraiche. Then the ricotta cheese will follow. Season with some chopped chives and some salt and pepper.
Over the crust, Flake Leftover smoked salmon. Place chives and capers on top. If needed, add a drizzle of olive oil on top.
Just serve. Enjoy! Enjoy!

Smoked Albacore Tuna Nicoise Salad

SERVING	PREP TIME	COOK TIME	PELLETS
6	6 HOURS	3 HOURS	PECAN

Dress up the greens for your fresh catch. Beautifully composed smoked albacore with potatoes, eggs, tomatoes, olives, green beans and lettuce drizzled with a red wine herbaceous vinaigrette.

INGREDIENTS:

6 Whole Tuna, steak
1 Cup salt
1 Cup brown sugar
1 Whole orange zest
1 Whole lemon zest
1/2 Pound Potatoes, new
1/4 Cup extra-virgin olive oil
1 Tablespoon salt
1/2 Tablespoon black pepper
1 Tablespoon Dijon mustard
1 Clove garlic
333/1000 Cup red wine vinegar
1 Teaspoon salt
1/4 Teaspoon black pepper
2 Tablespoon chopped flat-leaf parsley
2 Tablespoon Tarragon, fresh
1 Tablespoon lemon juice
1 Cup extra-virgin olive oil
6 Whole eggs
1/2 Pound Green Beans, fresh
1 Head butter lettuce
1/4 Cup Castelvetrano Olives, Pitted and Halved
2 Whole Fennel, bulb
1/2 Cup Cherry tomatoes, sliced
To Taste Radishes
To Taste Bean Sprouts, fresh

DIRECTIONS:

To make the brine, blend the salt, sugar and citrus zest in a small cup. Layer the brine and fish in a jar to ensure that there is adequate brine between each fillet if the fillets are stacked, so that the individual fillets do not touch. Let the fridge sit in the brine for 6 hours.

Set the temperature to 180 ° F when ready to cook and preheat for 15 minutes with the lid closed.

Remove from the brine fillets and rinse the excess. Pat, dry and put in the refrigerator on a cooking rack for 30-40 minutes. Remove the fillets from the refrigerator and cook directly on the grill for around 3 hours.

Increase the temperature to 225 ° F and cook for an additional hour or until a light brown color and flakes with a fork have formed in the fish.

Take it off the grill and let it cool to room temperature. Increase the temperature on the grill to 375 ° F and preheat when the tuna is cooling.

Toss the olive oil, salt , and pepper with the fresh potatoes. Put the potatoes in a half-sheet pan and cook for 20-30 minutes or until tender on the grill. Take it off the grill and let it cool to room temperature.

To make the dressing: In a blender, mix all the ingredients except for the olive oil, and puree until smooth. When the mixture is smooth, slowly pour the oil into the medium-high blender until everything is applied. With no separation, it should be emulsified absolutely. Set aside the dressing.

To make eggs: In a medium-sized saucepan, place the eggs and fill them with enough water to cover them. Place over medium-high heat for seven minutes and bring to a boil. Remove from the heat and put the eggs immediately to cool in ice water. Peel the eggs and reserve them.

Add water to a medium saucepan and bring to a boil. Garnish with green beans and cook for 5 minutes. Strain and put the green beans to cool in ice water. Reserve. Reserve.

Place the broken butter lettuce leaves in the bottom of the bowl and arrange on top of the bowl the following: potatoes, olives, fennel, cherry tomatoes, green beans, half-baked eggs, smoked albacore tuna, and sprouts of radish.

Drizzle and serve with dressing. Enjoy! Enjoy!

Sweet Smoked Salmon Jerky

SERVING	PREP TIME	COOK TIME	PELLETS
6	12 HOURS	6 HOURS	MAPLE

Give a sweet twist to a smoked salmon recipe & turn it into a hearty snack. Our jerky recipe will fulfill any savory cravings with brown sugar and a few hours in the smoker.

INGREDIENTS:

2 Quart water
3/4 Cup kosher salt
1/4 Cup Morton Tender Quick Home Meat Cure
4 Cup brown sugar
1 Cup maple syrup
3 Pound Wild Caught Salmon Fillet, skinned, pin bones removed
1 Cup maple syrup
1/4 Cup water

DIRECTIONS:

Combine the water, salt, soothing salt (if used), brown sugar and 1 cup of maple syrup in a big non-reactive dish. To dissolve the salt and sugar, stir with a long-handled spoon.

Slice the salmon into 1/2 " thick slices with the short side parallel to you on the cutting board with a sharp, serrated knife. In other words , make cuts from the end of your head to the end of your tail. (If the fish is frozen, this is considerably easier.)

Cut each strip crosswise into lengths of 4 "or 5".

Immerse the strips in the brine by measuring them with an ice sheet or plastic bag. Cover and refrigerate for 12 hours with plastic wrap.

Set the temperature to 180 ° F when ready to cook and preheat for 15 minutes with the lid closed.

Drain and discard the brine with the salmon strips. Arrange the salmon strips directly on the grill grate in a single layer. Smoke for a few hours (5 to 6), or until dry but not rock-hard jerky. When you bite into it, you want it to yield.

Combine the remaining cup of maple syrup with 1/4 cup of warm water halfway through the smoking process and brush the salmon strips with the mixture on all sides.

Transfer to a resealable plastic bag when it is still hot for the jerky. At room temperature, let the jerky rest for an hour. Squeeze some air from the bag and cool the jerky in the fridge. Enjoy! Enjoy!

Baked Halibut
Sandwich with Smoked Tartar Sauce

SERVING	PREP TIME	COOK TIME	PELLETS
4	10 MINS	30 MINS	HICKORY

We are going to take the fillet o 'fish to the next level. Two fresh brioche buns, tomatoes, lettuce and slathered with a smoked tartar sauce are loaded into Hickory roasted halibut.

INGREDIENTS:

1 Cup mayonnaise
1/2 Cup Pickles, chopped
1 Tablespoon Capers, chopped
1/2 Tablespoon parsley, chopped
1/2 Tablespoon Dijon mustard
1/2 lemon juice
6 thick-cut halibut fillets
To Taste salt and pepper
6 Brioche Bun
2 heirloom tomato
As Needed romaine lettuce heart

DIRECTIONS:

Start the Traeger grill when ready to cook and set the temperature to 180 degrees F (with Super Smoke allowed if a WiFIRE enabled grill is used) and preheat for 10 to 15 minutes, with the lid closed.

Combine in a small bowl all the tartar sauce ingredients, then spread on a shallow sheet tray and put directly on the pan grill.

Smoke for 20-30 minutes at 180 degrees F or until the appropriate amount of smoke flavor has been picked up by the tartar sauce. Move to the fridge and set aside until the halibut is ready.

Boost the temperature of the grill to 450 degrees F and preheat for 10-15 minutes with the lid closed.

Add salt and pepper to season the fillets and put on a sheet tray. Directly put the sheet tray on the grill grill and cook for 7-10 minutes or until the temperature inside reaches 145 degrees F.

Place cut side down brioche buns directly on the grill grill for 3 minutes to toast.

Spread some of the tartar sauce on each side of the bun to create the sandwich, then stack the fillet, sliced tomato and lettuce in the desired order on the bottom bun. Top and enjoy with top bun!

CPSIA information can be obtained
at www.ICGtesting.com
Printed in the USA
BVHW010544090421
604475BV00014B/1654